MURPHY'S LAW
TO
ENLIGHTENMENT

How to Do Everything Wrong
and Still Turn Out Alright

MURPHY'S LAW
TO
ENLIGHTENMENT

How to Do Everything Wrong
and Still Turn Out Alright

STORIES ABOUT LEARNING THROUGH FAILURES

CARY T. KELLEMS

ML
MARILEE
Publishing

ML
MARILEE
Publishing

Murphy's Law to Enlightenment: How to Do Everything Wrong and Still Turn Out Alright

MARILEE Publishing
PO Box 238, Altadena, CA 91003-0238
www.marileepublishing.com

ISBN-13: 978-1-7322482-3-6 (Paperback)

Library of Congress Control Number 2020938335

Chief Editor: Cynthia Gellis
Cover Design: Faiza Ahmed

Printed in the U.S.A.
First Printing, 2020

Ordering Information: Special discounts are available for volume purchases by schools, corporations, associations, and others. To place an order, call (562) 548-2284 or contact publisher at the address above.

This book reflects the authors' present recollections of observations and personal experiences over time. Some names and characteristics have been changed to protect the innocent or guilty, and some dialogue and events have been compressed. Both the publisher and author(s) regret any unintentional harm resulting from the book.

First Edition

DEDICATION

To my wife, Marge, and sons, Shawn and Gavin, who told me to shut up and write my stories down.

To my mom, who taught me sacrifice, and my dad who taught me grit.

To my brothers and sisters, who taught me everything a kid could learn during our sojourns from coast to coast to coast to coast.

To my friends who listen like what I said meant something.

ACKNOWLEDGMENTS

To Dr. Marion Somers who saw this book before I did.

To my publisher, David Kitchen, who convinced me that I could write a book.

To Roughwriters Toastmasters, who gave me encouragement that sustained me during the journey.

And to Roxanne, who plied me with extra shots of espresso so that I could complete it.

TABLE OF CONTENTS

PREFACE   ix

INTRODUCTION   xi

CHAPTER 1 | ACCEPTANCE
Float or Swim   3
An Old Friend   7
CHAPTER 2 | GRIT
The Gray Race   12
Souvenirs from the Journey!   15
Chasing Kites   18
Strength in the Darkness Before the Dawn   21
North to Alaska   24
CHAPTER 3 | DEATH
Phoenix   32
Death's Book of Secrets   35
Death Abides   39
CHAPTER 4 | FAITH
Options   42
The Wanderer   46
Darwin's Pool   49
CHAPTER 5 | AWARENESS
A Nerd, a Stoner, and a Prom Queen   54
Roadside   57
Postcards from Alaska   59
The Reason for Pain   62
Dark, Thin Silhouette   66

CHAPTER 6 | INTEGRITY

Play Your Hand   70

Moonshadow   73

True Identity   78

Tiny Green Army Men   82

Bright Eyes   86

CHAPTER 7 | INNER STRENGTH

My Last Redoubt   90

Creativity   96

CHAPTER 8 | PERSONAL GROWTH

Canvas   100

Three Doors   103

Just One More   106

Weightless   108

Lessons From A Bloody Nose   111

Long Bar   114

EPILOGUE | THIS BAR   117

ABOUT THE AUTHOR   119

PREFACE

Life is full of lessons, but am I the only one that got Professor Murphy for this class? Granted, I was not a particularly good student, but the assignments that Professor Murphy metered out were downright tricky. And to exacerbate the situation, when bad things happened to me, I took it as a dare to double down. I stubbornly continued to repeat my last mistake, always expecting a different result. Yep, a sure sign of insanity. Wash, rinse, and repeat. My life was in an infinite loop of mistakes with never a reflection of why bad things kept happening to me. Thank God for boredom.

Boredom manifested itself as the wise old guide who introduced me to the long road of enlightenment. It was in that moment of boredom that I began to revisit my past.

Boredom reached critical mass when I was a day clerk in a country liquor store. After my routine tasks of stocking the shelves, dusting the bottles, and sweeping the floors, I'd just loiter behind the cash register waiting for the next patron to push open the double doors. To break this monotony, I would take the discarded cigarette cartons and rip them lengthwise, which produced a clean white writing surface on one side and the cigarette manufacturers' logo on the backside. When a customer entered the store, I'd just cram this rigid writing pad into my back pocket. You'd see me walking around the store with the Marlboro or Kool's logo protruding from my butt pocket. Yet as soon as I heard the door close and the store was empty, you'd find me head down, leaning over the front counter writing.

I'd write whatever came to my mind. It started with a simple to-do list then blossomed into pages of personal rants, and eventually, it morphed into observations of the colorful patronage that frequented the liquor store. You know there might have even been a poem or two along the way, but every day I would fill up at least one 4.5 x 10-inch carton paper. When I got home, I'd open a drawer, throw them, and then close it.

I never revisited those notes. They had served their purpose. They had got me through the boredom, but they had also provided me with the briefest insight into the world around me and a serendipitous view into my own life.

Writing for myself became a habit. In college, I wrote much less. Having children, I wrote even less. Stress, anger, or pain would always draw me back to the psychiatrist's couch of my journals. It allowed me to find a new perspective if only I had been a better student. Even though my medium changed from cigarette cartons to a wire-bound notebook to handsome journals, then back to write in wire-bound notebooks again, the modus operandi was always the same. Write, rewrite then forget it.

Most of my writing was overflowing with the flotsam and jetsam of ordinary life. Yet, as my daddy taught me, "Son, we are too soon old and too late smart."

I have no recollection of when or why I started to page back through my old journals, but as I re-read them, patterns emerged. My habit of "wash, rinse, repeat," came into focus. After all those years, the psychiatrist within my journals spoke.

This book is full of stories that I have revisited. In going back, I have learned lessons, truths, and dare I say, enlightenment. Lesson learned under the adage of, "Better late than never!"

In reading these stories, see them for what they are, an invitation for you to take pen to paper, computer to a printer, thoughts to the internet. You have the power to document the events of your life and from your stories distill the most fabulous elixir of them all, enlightenment.

Thank you, Professor Murphy, for never giving up on your humble student.

INTRODUCTION

In all the world and for all times, there is only ever just one you. So how come society believes that we are all extruded from the same container of playdough. We are indoctrinated into a culture that expects us to be good little automatons. And when we fail to meet someone else's expectations, we feel ourselves failures.

My mind was a parfait of other people's expectations, my parents, my professors, and my perversion of societal expectation. My ability to cope with the contradiction of living the life of others' expectations could never wholly quench my thirst to drink the real me, the REAL me. Who was the real me?

This book is my journey to answer that question. How to discover the real me, the true you, the real us?

Examine your life with a survivalist's eye. Everything that went wrong provides you with enough evidence to make you the best you.

In the wild, if your trap fails to provide you with a meal, then it's up to you to either own it or starve. Murphy knew the best way forward often involves falling flat on your face.

From experience, I can tell you that as you lay flat on your face, its merely Murphy's gentle touch reminding you to pay attention to a particular life lesson and pointing you towards enlightenment.

Your personal stories are your unique path towards your peak of insight. Your accounts will guide you up the narrow roads and treacherous cliffs to the wizened guru who sits atop. In writing your story, you'll discover what I uncovered — that by the time you reach the peak, you'll find that the guru atop the mountain is you. Introspection, combined with the courage to look unflinchingly at the black and white of your own words, will ignite a level of understanding that will take you one step closer to the top.

Writing is like learning to ride a bike. At first, you'll focus on balance, power, and control. Every muscle, including your brain, is consumed with the task of not falling. Then, sometime during that first week after the training wheels are removed, you'll reflectively wave to a friend as you are riding. As you take your hand off the handlebars, the bike will wobble, and you'll quickly return your hand for full control. Eventually, your bike will become an extension of yourself. It will just be a tool to travel through a vast world. And so, it will be with your writing. The mechanics will give way to your why. Your stories will take on their own life, a life that will enrich you. Let these stories be your invitation to add your voice to this growing chorus. We are all better when we all share our stories.

Read and see that from looking back, we can grow forward.

CHAPTER 1:

ACCEPTANCE

Survival of the fittest is the law of the wild. This law was reinforced every day at the all-boys high school I attended. Although I never actually experienced a single lion, tiger, or bear in the hallway of my school, the natural pecking enforced the lesson of anger and resistance, and these emotions were powerful tools in my hand. But us against them, me against you, was the only tool in my tool chest, and as comfortable as resistance felt in my hand, I had to learn the hard way that other tools existed. That acceptance is a short cut to avoid the escalation of us versus the world.

It has always been so. From the moment we crawled out from the primordial ooze, we fought to survive, and then there was high school. You remember high school, where standing out was seldom a good idea. In my case, I didn't quite stand out as much as I stood below. Being one of the smallest kids in the class at an all-boys high school made me a perfect target. Just walking down the hallways would somehow invite a random chest-thumping from some senior. But I was not demure; against all reason, I reacted with anger and aggression. I never accepted it. I never forced down my eyes. My stare would let them know that I was ready, that I knew the danger, and that I would not be coward down. It didn't stop me from being thumped, but it somehow mitigated the pain of the punches. But aggression is not a long-term game plan, and acceptance is often a counter-intuitive alternative for long term survival. A lesson that life is just itching to teach us.

Float Or Swim

Now is the time!!...Oops gone again!

It was a stormy January morning at South Mission Beach. My best friend, Mark, and I stood looking around at the deserted beach. No birds, no lifeguards, only the windblown sand and the thundering 12-foot waves that crashed with a cadence like the galley drums aboard a Roman warship.

To this tune of doom, we donned our wetsuits and waded into the 54-degree water to body surf those massive waves. These were not the waves you see on the cover of Surfer magazine. Oh no, they were turgid beasts born from the breath of Dave Jones himself.

More excited than daunted, we slipped on our fins and began to swim out. As each wave approached, we dove deep and swam hard, surfacing just long enough to gulp some air – swim, dive, gulp, and repeat.

In rhythm with the oncoming waves, we repeated this exercise until we reach the final breakers. (An area just before the twelve-foot bone crushers.) In that ruthless zone, there is no time to contemplate. With every ounce of remaining energy, I would swim straight down. Deeper and deeper into the belly of the moving monster, hoping that I could make it under the impact of the marine guillotine above. And if I was lucky enough to reach the sandy bottom before the concussion of the waves, then I'd begin to crawl, piercing the ocean floor with my fingers and pulling my body against the onshore current until I experienced the reverberation of the crashing wave. Even at twelve feet below the surface, the wave's concussion bounced me like a spineless doll off the sandy bottom.

Quickly reorienting, I swam towards the surface, rising within a constellation of bubbles. Breathless, I broke the surface and gasped a gulp of spray that tasted of success. It was only then, and it was only there that I had my first opportunity to relax. I floated and began to study the swells that rolled beneath me. These swells bobbed me along in a slow-motion rodeo ride on the back of a massive slippery serpent. Up then down, I floated until the ocean and I were one symbiotic being. That was when it was time to strike. Catching the next swell, I kicked and stroked toward the shore, toward the apex of that breaker, toward a twelve-foot plunge down a moving mountain of water.

As I breached the crest, the offshore breeze spewed the froth of this monster wave in my face. With my vision obscured, I picked the best course and started my descent.

The buoyancy of my wetsuit and the sheer speed of my descent allowed my body to race virtually frictionless down the face of the glassy wave. My eyes became camera shutters to clear my vision of the spray. Each snapshot, the seascapes changed.

Snapshot one: the wave appears to stretch before me like a sheet of molten green glass.

Snapshot two: My speed triples, and I feel my long, wet hair flap behind my head as I reach the bottom.

Snapshot three: At full velocity, I skip like a neoprene stone over the swells.

Snapshot four: I start to slow until I crash into the next swell.
One thousand one, one thousand two, one thousand three, one thousand four; that's all I get. Just four heartbeats to enjoy that suicidal ride.

As my heart struck its fifth beat, the chilly Pacific breaker buried me in a watery tomb. Down, down, down I went, until my body was pinned between twelve feet of water and the ocean's sandy floor.

I attempted to push off the bottom, but the weight of the wave felt like the burden of ten thousand drowned souls. Those death thralls fertilized my fear. Their perishing panic became my panic, and I started to struggle like a caged animal. I mindlessly beat myself against the wet bars of an invisible cage.

My whole life, I've railed against life's cages. Whether those bars were physical or metaphysical, I'd leave each encounter either boastful or bloodied.

As I struggled, I felt the oxygen start to dissipate from my muscles. My mind screamed all the louder; I can do it; I can beat this. Just one more push and I would throw the world of water from my shoulders because it had always been me versus the world.
I would overcome it.
I could succeed.
I can't.

No amount of exertion would extricate me from this watery fate. A sense of failure matching the depth triggered my mind to twitch and scurry, looking for ways to resist. At that moment of terror, something new bloomed.

My oxygen deprivation induced a narcotic state that quelled the animal urge to fight. In its place, flowered the wonder to accept the predicament.

At that moment, I granted the ocean sway over my life. This permission allowed my body to relax and give full reign to the strong currents. The ocean rolled me along its sandy floor. Acceptance vanquished my panic and nourished my mind with oxygen that flowed from the relaxed state.

If these were to be my last moments, why waste them on fear? I open myself up to experience, whatever was to be. I let my taut muscles go limp. I gave fate full providence. In the contest between life and death, acceptance won.

As my body rolls beneath these deep currents, I suddenly felt the ocean release its grasp. This new freedom offered me a single shining opportunity to survive. I instinctively pushed off the bottom and started to swim to the surface.

It became a race for air. I swam for oxygen and life. It was a race between consciousness and oxygen. I instinctually knew that I had just one chance for air. If I was unlucky and broke the surface only to gulp in saltwater, the ocean would pull me down into its cold bosom.

Struggling hard to concentrate, I attempted to remember which direction the coast was. I knew that I had to be facing the sandy beach to ensure that some unseen waves did not drown my last opportunity for air. No time left, I make my best guess and throw the dice. Moments before my head broke the surface, I exhaled all my remaining breath, betting my life that the next inhale would be full of air and not salty brine.

My head popped up amongst the chaos of fallen waves. I quickly gulped air just as a smaller wave crashed down on me. That wave pushed me down again. But then I am in a state of giddy calmness. With my body revitalized with fresh air, I waited patiently for a chance to resurface.

Surfacing again in the relative calm before the massive breakers, I relaxed. My breathing began to match the rhythm of the rolling waves. As I floated, I allowed the blood to rush back into every part of my body. Starring up from a rolling world into a roiling sky, I had the luxury to ponder lessons of exhilaration, death, and acceptance.

Invigorated from my struggle in the world of crashing waves, would I continue to float? Or would I muster the bold audacity to catch the next wave that would hurtle me over the falls to either be thrown down to the bottom or flung like a rock to skip and skim before the crashing wave?

Stay and float, or swim and ride. It was my Sisyphean dilemma that I asked as I looked up at the gray, racing sky.
What would I do?
Float or swim.
What do you do?
Float or swim. Float or SWIM!!

An Old Friend

Old friends are like a warm blanket, best when you are cold.

My mother's admonition, "You'll be known by the friends that you keep," never rang more true than when I opened my front door and discovered one of my oldest, though far from dearest, friends.

His time-worn face betrayed a lifetime of disappointments, and his hobbled gait betrayed a lifetime of misfortune. He eagerly took the seat I offered him, and we began reminiscing about the old days.

The very first time I met him, I was merely five years old. We were living in naval housing at Norfolk Naval Base in Virginia. "We" was my mom and dad, my two older sisters, and my newborn baby brother. It was on account of said baby brother that I found myself outside being "supervised" by my older sisters who, on my best days, found me only mildly annoying. You know how it is with younger brothers.

Surrounding our government-supplied housing was a forest. And on that fateful day, I ventured into its cool shadows. I paused to look up at the forest shadows before me, then broached its dark canopy.

Within the confines of the forest, I experienced an array of flora and fauna that included daddy-long-legs, beetles of every shape and color, and mosses like rare Persian carpets. I experienced the sheer joy of rambling over and under the fallen logs and shrubs. Each step was like opening a new treasure chest of boyhood wonder. Each treasure pulled me deeper within its dark canopy until I became lost in the forest showcase, lush with heavy shadows and spires of piercing light.

In that moment of disorientation and desperation, I first met my oldest, though not dearest friend. A friend called Fear. Fear dined on my immaturity and made my heart ring in my ears. I panted for air as I whirled around, desperately searching for a way home. Fear only watched and smiled. It was the haunting smile you'd find on the face of a broken clown figurine.

I called out for my sisters.

I cried out for my mother.

I cried out until someone found me.

Fear followed me when I said goodbye to my Norfolk friends and we moved to Long Beach, California. He followed when I said goodbye to my Long Beach friends and moved to Jacksonville, Florida. He even followed when I said goodbye to my Jacksonville friends and moved back to San Diego, California. I hated him, but my hatred only tightens our bonds. He was always there.

Living in San Diego, I had the great fortune to be surrounded by a vast wilderness of sagebrush and sandstone cliffs. I could hike for miles and miles in those pre-teen days of endless energy. One hot morning, I came across two storm drains that ran about 80 feet under Navajo Road.

I remember peering down those dark throats and imagining myself the discoverer of a fantastic shortcut. I started to shimmy down the left pipe. It was a snug fit. I made progress by synchronizing the pull of my outstretched hands and the push of my toes. I progressed about halfway down that storm drain, then no further. I was stuck.

A thin layer of dried sediments between my toes and the smooth cement drain stopped my progress, and the light at the end of the tunnel stretched into infinity. I thrashed about like a headless rattlesnake, but I only became more immobile. Stuck! As this realization fell over me, my flesh began to flush. My mouth felt dry, yet my hands were clammy. I was being consumed whole by claustrophobia. I was in the belly of the beast. I couldn't breathe. I couldn't move. Bound by my old friend Fear.

I began to drown in the still waters of panic. I could not go forward; I could not go back. It was there in the cool air of that storm drain, moments before asphyxiation or hyperventilation that I made my peace with Fear. In that instant, as Fear took me to the edge of life, I learned that my aversion to Fear was his strength. The more I fought the biological influences, the more invincible Fear became. It was in that cold, dank darkness that I accepted Fear and all his machinations. And with acceptance, Fear slowly melted away.

I slowed my breathing. I relaxed. After several attempts, I began to slide myself back down the last forty feet of that storm drain.

Upon exiting that large pipe, I filled my lungs in the warm morning air. I stood there dirty, sweaty, and smiling.

I had finally vanquished my rivalry with Fear. Fear was no longer debilitating; Fear became exhilarating. We climbed rock cliffs; we braved chaotic surf, we hurled ourselves from safety again and again. If we had the opportunity, we would have taken selfies together. Never again would he hold sway as he did those many years ago amongst the dark and lonely trees in Virginia.

As we sat there in my living room and recapped all my close escapes, Fear kept muttering, "But you coulda' died, Cary. You could have died!"

I let the silence grow and then replied, "You're right, but that's how you taught me to live!"

You know, my mom always said, "You'll be judged by the friends you keep."

Keep them close!!

CHAPTER 2:

GRIT

Grit is the taskmaster that keeps beating you as you reply, "Thank you, sir, may I have another!" Climbing up a mountain of sand that charges a toll of a single step for every two steps that you take, it's grit that powers you through that Sisyphean task. It is the heart-thumping satisfaction that screams from your burning lungs as you crest the dune. Grit is a muscle that you build by never shying away from frustrating events, people, and tasks. When the going gets tough, you don't ask, "Why me?" You ask, "What lesson can I learn?" In every breath, there is a lesson. In every broken bone, there is a lesson. In every broken heart, there is a lesson. That lesson is grit.

Where does grit grow? It grows in the fields of frustration, in the darkness when you know that no one will come, and in the pursuit of an ideal. When you fall and get a face full of dirt, it's grit that powers you to stand up, spit out the earth and the blood and finish the damn race. Then and only then, will you know the satisfaction of the man in the arena who strives mightily.

The Gray Race

The problem with clones is how do you determine who's gonna be the designated driver and how do you tell them that you haven't picked any of them to be your best man.

I was thirty years old, and I was lost, lost in a desert wasteland, the desert wasteland of the corporate cubicle farm. It was there where I began to resemble a pot-bellied prairie dog. Like whack-a-moles, we'd pop our heads above the cubicle walls, Hey Bob, do you smell cake? I think someone brought cake. I smell cake, Bob...where's the cake, Bob? Eventually, I realized that this sedentary, cake-filled existence was not for me. Spurred to take some sort of action, I started to run.

Running became my daily battle between pain and will, then a daily struggle between will and pain. Eventually, my emigrant soul persevered. Faster, farther, and longer, I ran until weeks became months. On my one year running anniversary, in the lingering coolness of some late spring morning, I glimpsed a gray-haired runner just cresting the very same hill I was about to ascend. As playful motivation, I swore to overtake the gentleman before we both came upon the next hill. I redoubled my pace. Yet my prey appeared no closer. I lengthened my stride, but I was still no closer. I cut every corner; I began to sprint, yet he again receded into the morning mist.

Month after month, this frustrating episode replayed, leaving me bent over in pain and puzzlement. I swore to myself; I'd beat him. I enhanced my running with strength training at the gym. I subscribed to running magazines. As I approached the second anniversary of my foray into running, I broke off the cast of a weekend warrior. I had remodeled myself into an athlete.

When the next Saturday rolled around, I was ready. I had released my inner hounds of war. I ran with reckless confidence. That is until I again saw my gray-haired nemesis just cresting the hill. I did not run up that hill, I bounded up it with all the confidence of a lion pouncing upon an injured prey, but as I crested the hill, I saw, much to my dismay, that my worthy opponent had a sizable lead. (Had he been training too?) No matter, in perfect form and substantial speed, I ran.

I ran fast enough to be cooled by my breeze. And I could see that I was catching up. Closer and closer, I strode, now only a block away. One gut-wrenching push, and there was just fifty feet between us. But no closer. As I relented, I gained that now-familiar sight of the gray-haired gentleman receding into the morning air. Never once did he even turn around to acknowledge my heroic struggle. Never once did he give me the satisfaction of knowing my foe's face.

The vision of him running off became my inspiration. As I strained in pain at the gym, I imagined him sneering and gloating.

Years multiplied into decades, and I still ran. I played running games with my children; I took my running gear on my business trips. I would sprint, and I would log long miles. And each runner I would encounter became a sublimated version of my gray-haired nemesis. I would never let anyone just run ahead of me. I needed to meet them stride for stride, to beat them.

In the dry dawn hours of one September morning, I started my run. My running regimen was a three-minute cycle. I would begin at a trot; then, for the next three-minute period, I would run; then three-minutes of full out sprint and back to trotting for three-minutes. I would repeat this pattern until I finished my loop. When I got to the hills, I again spied my gray-haired nemesis. I broke from my prescribed cycle and just sprinted flat out. With efficiency, grace, and ease, I gained ground. I strategized and flowed toward my prey. Mile after mile until, in utter disbelief, I caught up to him. In the few strides, before I passed him, I composed myself by adjusting my pace, regulating my breathing, and wiping the sweat from my brow.

As I passed him, I eagerly glanced back to see the face of my tormentor. To gain the satisfaction that had taken me decades to accomplish. Yet as our eyes locked, he disappeared. All that remained behind me was a young runner off in the distance, a younger runner trying to catch up, trying to catch me, a gray-haired man who was running ever faster.

Souvenirs From The Journey

Don't put off until tomorrow because the odds are no longer in your favor.

Age is the journey. Experiences are the souvenirs we collect along the way. Wisdom is the alchemist who blends these experiences in the proper proportions to transform us from a youthful tourist into an enlightened traveler.

Unfortunately for me, the alchemist cannot seem to get the proportions correct, as in, the mind is willing, yet the body is less forgiving. As we age, everyone, everything, and every part of our body tells us it's time to stop; it's time to relax. Like the Siren's call, beckoning us towards the rocks of retirement, it serenades us with promises of lotus petal dreams that only quicken us towards a cairn grave.

Many of my friends tempt me to eat the lotus flowers of reminiscing. (So sweet, so tasty, so debilitating.) Now I have never been a party to such demeaning drivel as the thought that you prepare all your life just to jettison it all away, like some flotsam on the open sea. It has taken me a lifetime to be the masterpiece I am today (my friends are always telling me what a piece of work I am), and now you all want me to retire from the living community of progress and purpose, to become a sterile seed floating on the wind?

I have the will and the desire to give. My values have not changed, yet my patience is depleting daily. So, I stash my crumpled plans in my pocket, and I dive into action. That's correct; I leap into battle without a plan, for only rash action can break the heavy chain of age. Contingencies replace youthful dreams as I fight for balance in the free fall.

Have your dreams been beaten out of you? If so, now is the time to act. Do anything — volunteer, join a club, or learn a new skill. But do, and in doing, you will naturally discover your internal compass, your true north.

Each revelation takes its pound of flesh but imparts a buoyant spirit that wants to elevate you and those around you. That is why at age sixty, I changed my life. Committing to change, I turned my back on a forty-year career of numbers and processes and looked to a calling of people and relationships.

The journey that aged me also altered me in other ways. From the base metals of analytical and uptight, I was transformed into a being with the golden purpose of assisting others in discovering themselves through personal stories. A mission that was simultaneously unfathomable and unreachable just a few short years ago now beckons me.

Looking out over a storm capped ocean, I force myself to see beyond my current circumstances, to an imaginary shore. On that distant shore, I stand feeling the warm sand between my toes. In my hand, I hold my first novel. Yet my focus is not upon the story in my hand; it is upon an even more distant shore where I visualize myself holding my next book. My dream is like a repetitive imagine within multiple mirrors; it goes on ad infinitum.

My journey has uncovered within me a voiceless prisoner hidden away in the labyrinths of my binary mind. From a career of bits and bytes, I have ventured out into the unknowable realm of relationships. Into this formless land, I bring along many of my old traits like my consuming enchantment for solving real-world puzzles, my love of learning, and my insatiable desire to accomplish personal milestones.

Journeys rearrange our very molecules. This barely begun journey has awoken in me a new vision. As I write this, I have taken the first of a million future steps. Who knows what souvenirs I'll collect? Who knows where it will lead?

With those questions in mind, I have begun to accept the wonder of a traveler in a new land.

Chasing Kites

Rain turns mountains into sand.

Taking the job that no one wants has been the key to my success. In my decades' long career at IBM, I discovered that opportunities abound in the workplace. You can find them under the rocks labeled dirty jobs.

At IBM, it started innocently enough. There was a critical application that required substantial changes. This application was full of what we called spaghetti code. No one wanted to touch it because there was no documentation for how it operated. Working on this application was akin to being dropped naked in the middle of the Amazon rainforest without a map on Monday and instructed to be in Los Angeles by eight a.m. on Friday. (And NO, that wasn't me in that Naked and Alone episode.)

The office legend was that any change to the code would bring this critical application crashing down. Incorrectly changing this application could kill your career. So why did I raise my hand to volunteer? Because patience and persistence were what powered me.

When I was a kid, the worst thing that could happen when you were flying your kite was for your string to break. Then you'd have to run at breakneck speed while looking straight up at a speck in the sky in an attempt to follow your kite as it fluttered back to the ground.

I would chase my falling kite through playgrounds, over fences, into backyards, and down the street to eventually find it trapped in some large tree.

When your string broke, it was the pits. So, you can imagine my joy in seeing that spool of nylon string sitting on the drugstore shelf for the first time. I thought it was the technological advancement that would revolutionize kite flying.

As soon as I had saved enough pennies, I purchased that spool of soft, spun nylon kite string. In my mind, I wasn't just buying kite string. I was purchasing the promise of ruling the kite flying skies!

I restrung my four-foot kite, and on the next windy day, I was ready. The strong wind ripped my kite from my hands. I felt the silky-smooth nylon string feed though my fingers, and in no time, my lime green kite was just a colorful comma in the clear blue sky. Higher, further, faster, it flew. My fellow kite flyers were in awe. I was the king of the heavens that day. Everyone wanted to know my secret. I showed them the future of kite flying. Behold! My spool of nylon string!

When it was time to go home, I began to bring my kite back to earth. I rewound the nylon string around its spindle, but it was slick and began to slip off the end into a tangled mess on the ground. Unlike regular line, the nylon string was very soft and very slippery. The more I wound, the more my new, nylon string resembled a rat's nest by my feet.

When I finally got my kite earthbound, I gathered it and my pile of nylon string and walked home dejected. In our garage, I began the task of rewinding my nylon string into a cohesive spool. The more I worked it, the more it would fray. With each rewind, I had to untangle and stretch the line to perform the simple task of making it stay on the spindle. Minutes became hours as I patiently rewound this mess.

My mom came by. "How is it going? Dinner will be ready soon."

I remember looking up at her with a mixture of frustration and determination.

"Almost got it."

But that was childish optimism. Dinner came, and I was still not done.

After dinner, I was back at it. By this time, the marvel of nylon string had lost all its luster. I was tired, but something in me would not give up until it was all rewound.

Late that night, I had restored my spool of string. With stubborn pride, I placed the spool back next to my lime green kite and went to bed.

As I fell asleep that night, a smile graced my face. Yes, I felt a satisfaction in a job well done, but it was more than that. Years later, I realized how that single event had changed me. How that day I planted a seedling that would mature into a tenacity to tackle any dirty job no matter how tangled it appeared.

Strength in the Darkness Before the Dawn

Find yourself in the darkness to be your best self after the dawn.

Just the other day, I saw a guy throwing telephone books onto everyone's front porch. Let me tell you, that took me back. Way back. Back to 1967.

Now 1967 wasn't the best of times; it wasn't the worst of times; it was just another time. A time when people would routinely leave their front doors open when they departed in the mornings just so that the house wouldn't be hot when they returned. It was a time when a kid would walk his dog without a leash, and every mother was your mother when your mother wasn't around. (When moms are everywhere, it is quite challenging to get away with anything.)

It was in that summer of 1967, just before I went into the seventh grade, that I became a paperboy for the San Diego Union. My wife now swears that it is because of that formative experience that I became a morning person. She may be right. Being a paperboy meant getting up every single morning at four. I'd walk outside and oh so quietly open our garage door. Just inside, I had all my supplies neatly stowed. There were my rubber bands to bind the folded paper together, the canvas bags to hold those folded papers, and of course, my trusty Phillips bike to transport me and my precious cargo.

When the white van embossed with San Diego Union arrived, my manager would drop off my bundles. I would get to work — snip the baling wire and start folding, banding, and stuffing my papers. Once I was done, I'd sling the canvas bags over the back of my bike, oh so quietly shut the garage door, and peddle off into the pre-dawn darkness.

My delivery route was a quarter of a mile from my home. I'd go up a short, steep hill, then down a long, straight one to my clients. My route fluctuated between eighty to one hundred houses, homes nestled next to a vast sagebrush wilderness know as Cowles Mountain.

When you ride your bike at four a.m., you experience the world in a hush. The neat rows of darkened homes looks downright post-apocalyptic. Imagine weaving in and out of driveways with barely a sound, startling herds of rabbits grazing on the sweet front lawns of suburbia. And on rare occasions, catching glimpses of coyote packs prancing down the long streets. As I peddled to each home, I would reach back, grab a paper, and sling the morning news. I was always aiming at the welcome mat yet occasionally finding a rack of empty milk bottles or that unfortunate sleeping cat instead.

Every morning, seven days a week, 365 days a year, I'd make that solitary trek. And for that dedication, I would make the rather princely sum of one dollar per customer per month. Yep, on a good month, I might make a hundred dollars. I can tell you, back then, that was a heck of a lot of money, especially for a kid whose sole vices were sodas, Slurpees, and model cars. I had money to spare. My folks opened a savings account for me. Within two years, I had accrued almost two thousand dollars.

It wasn't just the money that got me up every morning. It was also the sweet taste of grit. It was the battle between preparation and fate. Alone, I learned how to put my chain back on the sprockets, fix flat tires, and dust myself off when I crashed. Whatever I encountered, I overcame it. I prevailed over escaped dogs, rainy days, and slick driveways. At four a.m., there is no village, no parents, nobody but me, a small twelve-year-old boy, alone in the darkness before the dawn.

There were mornings when I had to push my bike back up that hill because it was unrideable, days when I had to take those canvas bags off the back of my bike and sling them over my shoulders to complete my route. It was me, the middle of five children who learned via fate and failure to forge a quiet confidence.

That two thousand dollars that I saved is long gone, along with the car and a dirt bike that I spent it on, yet that quiet confidence, that grit, has only grown more persistent during the intervening years.

Alone, each of us confronts the hills of life. Take this moment to look back at the corners of your own life, and there you'll discover the forge that shaped you.

Those events might have been the best of times; those events might have been the worst of times, but they were your time. A time that forged the workpiece for your today and all your tomorrows.

North to Alaska

You can look at the map, or you can look down at the footprints that follow you wherever you go

I was languishing in that post-college quagmire where your life forks toward infinite paths. It was a time of indecision, so I punted. I decided to go on vacation. That fateful non-decision taught me the difference between tourist and traveler, the difference between destination and journey. But before I begin, a brief prolog is in order:

I had just rebuilt my Datsun 510. I had the heads re-milled, and the cylinders bored out. Like a surgeon under the hood, I called, "Spanner wrench," and my assistant replied, "Spanner wrench."

Next, "spline alignment tool."

Igor (er Bob) replied, "spline alignment tool."

Then "gear puller."

"Gear puller," echoed back.

"Ring compressor."

"Ring compressor."

O.K., Igor...err Bob.... throw the switch. The Datsun roared to life.

"It's alive; it's alive!"

I had created my own post-modern, street racer. During my first test drive, I sped up the steepest road. My baby whined to a perfect automotive pitch. Beaming with pride, I started back down.

Spying the traffic light at the bottom of the hill, I eased on the brakes. They did not work. Instead of slowing the hills decline pushed me faster towards the red light and the lone Volkswagen waiting for the light to turn green. I felt my heart in my throat.

I forcefully downshifted. My newly reborn car whined in pain as the tachometer spike into the danger zone. I pumped and pumped the brakes. Now in full panic, I applied the emergency brake, then downshifted again. I was slowing, but it would not be enough. But wait, the light turned green. I was going to make it; I was going to make it. Why wasn't that Volkswagen moving??? The light was green but no movement from the VW. I downshifted for the last time, and the VW slogged ahead with the fits and starts of a newborn's first steps...I pulled on the emergency brake with all that I could, but BAM! Impact.

After I squared accounts with the woman who was driving her son's VW, my best friend John and I packed up the Datsun and drove north from San Diego. North to Alaska. We traveled up the coastal highways, always keeping the blue pacific on our left and a forgotten America on our right. We grazed upon smoked salmon, Tillamook cheese, and washed it down with a tour of the Olympia Brewery. We stopped in towns with only one traffic light and a single diner. Sitting at the diner bar in one such establishment, the waitress graced us with coffee, yet eyed us as strangers. Her nametag read Zona, and that said it all. We took our pie to go. We slept under the evergreen canopy of the North Cascades, which were under the clouds, which were under the stars.

At the Canadian border, the guards scrutinized me, a leaping gnome with long, blonde hair, with high suspicion until their search of my car revealed two skateboards.

"What's this aboot?"

Why for riding in Alaska.

"Suoo ya gonna ride in Alaska, aaah?"

25

Not fully understanding their strange language, I just nodded my head in agreement.

They let us go, and we continued north to Alaska.

We sampled the beautiful, Canadian countryside as we drove. Its coastal inlets, lush forests, and quaint towns all contributed to a trip back in time.

We eventually made our way to the Al-Can highway. Built during World War II, it connects Canada with Alaska. And traveling upon it, you'll swear that a drunken sailor on ice skates designed it. Within the first quarter-mile of the dirt and gravel road, under the sleepy eyes of dusk, I nearly crashed head-on into a car full of drunken lumberjacks who shined so bright that they had failed to turn on their headlights. I pulled to the side of the highway so we could collect our breath and finish our curses when John and I noticed the burned-out bones of an eighteen-wheeler. Melted tires, shattered windows, and draped in a black pallor, the truck and its trailer looked like a decaying brontosaurus. Being young men, we saw no omens, just a cool wreck. We continued with the very same certainty that General Custer had as he entered Little Bighorn.

We soon discovered that the road's primary use — as a transportation corridor for the logging industry. These massive eighteen-wheelers would pull as many as three trailers filled to overflowing with tree trunks. As these behemoths passed us on this two-lane gravel road, we would become engaged in a game of dodge ball. The trucks would kick-up gravel at sixty miles per hour, and we would pass them at sixty miles per hour. At the intersection of these two tangents, our objective was to dodge the iron ore butterflies that seemed to hang in the air as if suspended on an artist's mobile.

We learned that daylight travel was a death-match that we could not win. So, we devised a new plan — we would travel at night! We would spend an entire day sleeping and then around three p.m. take off north, north to Alaska.

Traveling under the stars was like moving between planets, no light, no life, only the road, and blackness. After a couple of days of our nighttime sojourns, the sky played a trick on us. We pulled off the highway, turned off our headlights, and witnessed the unsettling awe of the Aurora Borealis. It expanded then shrank across the inky, star-speckled canvas of the sky. Our minds returned to the campfire of our cave-dwelling ancestors who looked up and were both frightened and amazed.

Although we were making good time, we grew anxious, and after an abbreviated sleep, we headed out during the daylight hours. It was raining intermittently, and the car handled like marbles on linoleum. I was driving through a sequence of tight switchbacks that had a cliff on one side and a steep incline on the other. I took the switchbacks way too fast.

We started skidding towards the cliff. I overcompensated, and we began slipping towards the bank. I corrected again, and again, we were sliding towards the cliff. I could not keep up this dance between cliff and embankment. I ran out of road and out of time.

I had jackknifed the car to such a degree that we were traveling backward down that cliff. I'll never forget the feeling, a Wyle Coyote moment. With one hand on the steering wheel and the other on the door handle, I braced for whatever came next. As we flipped backward, all I could see was the brown embankment give way to patchy skies.

I said to John, "Here we go!"

In the blink of an eye, the car flipped and twisted backward, end-over-end, hurtling toward the raging river below. The whirlwind ended in a "Thud."

Still dazed, I asked John, "You okay?"

John replied, "I think so."

As my senses caught up to my now stationary body, I turned to John, "Your head is bleeding."

John wiped his forehead with his hand and replied, "Just a flesh wound."

27

I then proceeded to check myself out and discovered I still had a death grip on the door handle. A door handle I had ripped off the door while the car was cartwheeling down the hill. A door handle, I still clutched in my frozen grip.

We had miraculously landed upright. The roof on the passenger side had collapsed. We had lost the front windshield, two tires had been torn off my custom wheels and, oh yes, and we were about a hundred feet down from the road and about twenty feet from the river below. A small grove of saplings had stopped our plummet into the river. John and I climbed out of the driver's side window and hiked up to the Al-Can highway.

We wait for forty-five minutes until someone drove by, and I mean they drove by; they did not stop! In the middle of actual nowhere, they drove right by us. We looked to see if we were standing by any hockey masks or a pile of rusty chain saws on the side of the road. But no, it was just John and me looking puzzled.

We waited for another thirty minutes until the next, kinder soul stopped and drove us thirty miles back down the road to the only source of life, a gas station garage. For the bargain price of every dollar in my wallet, they brought out their tow truck — a tow truck designed to tow eighteen-wheelers. We returned to the scene of the accident. We had to cut the saplings down so that we could wrench my car up from the river's edge.

Eventually, we got it back to the garage. There we were able to duct tape the windshield back into position and reattach and inflate the tires. With the help of a small juice can and some o-clamps, we were able to reconnect the exhaust system.

In that condition, my beloved Datsun was able to take us from the mile marker 492 to Anchorage, Alaska, a trip of over a thousand miles. Yes, we got some strange looks at the border crossing. Yes, the car sounded more like a tank than my beloved street racer. But it did bring us to our new home in Anchorage, Alaska.

Despite the omens, John and I stayed in Alaska for over a year and made lots of new friends. We saw land that defies simple classification. It is an area so vast and empty that when you venture into its void, you believe that you are the first human to leave a footprint. The first human to take back a memory of its specific beauty.

Go there, be a traveler, and become local to the exotic. And with each footstep you make, you'll look down at that imprint and know that the journey is the destination.

CHAPTER 3:

DEATH

Standing graveside causes your body to wrench in pain and loss, yet for all this sorrow, funerals are for the living. They give us the opportunity for closure. Death, earth, and rebirth, then enlightenment? After all this, do we get it? I mean, does someone have to die? You'd have to be dense not to get it then, right? Death is a very patient teacher, and eventually, we will all learn its lessons or become its lesson for others to learn.

Death is the professor whose course is titled "How to Live a Better Life," even if no one ever passes its final exam.

Phoenix

Death leaves shadows of love on our grieving souls

Phoenix will not rise again. The cold earth will take her into its bosom. Into the meticulously dug grave, we laid her body down onto a bed of freshly picked honeysuckle.

We all looked down at her, wrapped in her favorite blanket. Then after what seemed like an eternity, we spontaneously began to tell the tale of her life and her significance to us.

Phoenix was never really our cat as much as we were her human litter. She took good care of us. Every night she would go to each of my sons' bedrooms and meow to be let in. Later she learned the trick to reach up to the levered door handles and let herself in. Once inside, she would demand her pets and scratches, then survey the room and exit to repeat the process in the next boy's room. She was checking up on each of us before she would allow herself to sleep. And if any boy were missing, then she would lay on his bed until he returned.

When my wife and I would walk around the block, there would be Phoenix, taking the point. She would skulk and dart before us, ensuring to herself that no danger lay ahead.

Phoenix started life as one of our neighbor's litter of five. We had no intention of getting a cat until that fateful day when the momma cat escaped their house with one of the very young kittens. Our entire block volunteered in the search for the momma and her bold kitten.

As fate would have it, my youngest son found the baby kitten. And, as they say, the rest is history.

Gavin named her Phoenix, for she had risen from oblivion, from lost to found. Phoenix was the only one of her litter that was polydactyl (she had an extra toe on each of her front paws). Her litter family all exhibited the bobtail of the Manx breed, yet Phoenix had a short, wiry tail.

Phoenix was a brilliant cat. She learned how to pop the screen door and let herself out. Maybe more impressively, with her Velcro-like polydactyl paws, she was able to open the screen door just enough to squeeze back into the house. For her, the world was a puzzle that was waiting to be solved.

In her prime, she was quite the huntress. Starting with lizards and mice, then moving up to the occasional rat, and eventually to birds. She would leave the remains of her victories so we could catalog them. One day she was at the back door with another prize, a blackbird, her nemesis. I opened the slider to congratulate her, and she strutted proudly into the house with the dead bird in her mouth.

Once inside, she dropped the vanquished bird at my feet and rubbed up against my leg to let me know she expected scratches and pets. As I was stroking her, I saw the dead bird stir. A distracted Phoenix just missed snatching the bird as it took flight. Once it was in the air, Phoenix took chase, and I was in the center of a cat-bird whirlwind. The bird was flapping and crashing into the ceiling, walls, and bookcases, with Phoenix manically in pursuit. The madness lasted until I could broom the flying bird out an open door.

We all learned to march to the beat of Phoenix's internal clock. Each morning, she would pop open my bedroom door, hop onto our bed, walk directly onto my chest, and sit down, silently demanding that it was time to let her out. Oh, and Phoenix's internal clock did not reset for daylight savings time.

She loved cheese, butter, and you could never leave bacon grease uncovered because she would lick it clean. But it was tuna fish in the can that would make her dance in expectation. When Marge made tuna salad, she would always save some of the juice for Phoenix.

A year ago, she was getting a bit ornerier, and we noticed a growth on her ears. When we took her to the Cat Clinic, we were not surprised to learn that she had cancer. The veterinarian said that she was pretty sure that she could save Phoenix but that she would have to remove her ears. As gruesome as it sounds, there was never a question about what to do. It took a while for all of us to get used to an earless cat. But true to form, Phoenix rose again. She was back to her spunky self. Running through the hallway and playing hide and seek.

Then about a month ago, while watching TV with us, Gavin noticed that she was panting as she rested. Within a week, her panting became an audible wheeze. So, we packed her back to the veterinarian.

The vet took about eight ounces of fluid out of Phoenix's chest cavity and warned us that it was either pneumonia or congestive heart failure. A few days later, the test came back. Her heart was failing. The vet's prognosis was shattering — Phoenix had about a month to live. Our instructions were, "Just make her comfortable."

As the days progressed, we brought her food and tuna juice. Each night we pulled her blanket next to the fireplace.

Then like a thief in the night, while Phoenix's family slept, she got up, crawled off into a hidey-hole in the office, and died.

Phoenix was a force of nature. A power that watched over us as we now watched over her as she laid silent and forever still.

Phoenix, we love you.

Death's Book of Secrets

When I die, I hope I'm a good read.

It was a typical November day, the sky was clear, the sun was warm, but the breeze was cool. I felt the chill as I walked across the cemetery.

It had been decades since I had visited the burial site, and if not for the willow tree, I might not have found it again. The willow's branches now encompassed the grave marker. I kicked them away.

Have you ever noticed the way that rows of grave markers in a cemetery resemble the book stacks of a library shelf? Each grave marker giving us only a glimpse of what transpired between the hyphenated dates that we see. The one I visited simply reads 1954 – 1978. And with your permission, I would like to open that book and reveal its secrets from death's library.

This book begins with a faded newspaper headline.

At eight twenty-five p.m. on November sixteenth, 1978, two young men met for the first time.

These two young men were the same age. Both had attended high school in the same city. One was on the football team, the other a wrestler. Their lives overflowed with laughter, dreams, and disappointments Six years had passed since those glory days, and each had moved on. One dreamed of graduating from college with a master's degree, the other dreamed of his next fix. One attended school by day and worked the night shift at a liquor store. The other worked days at a machine shop and worked nights supporting an escalating heroin habit.

The machine shop was windowless; the garage door was the only entrance for light or wind. Years of burnt oil and grease stained the shop floor. On hot afternoons, the air inside the shop was stifling.

This young man was the gopher, the grunt, the shop lackey. As the brunt of the older men's cruel jokes, he began to know each man by the shoes they wore. He was not part of a team; he was merely the water boy, the shop idiot who hurried around for the amusement of others.

At night, the liquor store was more like a well-lit fishbowl. It was conveniently located just down the hill from the university, serving both the student body and the school administrators. Occasionally, a beach bum would stumble in to purchase a bottom shelf bottle, replete with a paper bag.

This young man knew his regulars by their faces and some by name. Around six-thirty, Father Mulroney strode in for some light banter and a bottle of Campari. Sometime later, the law students would come in for some top-shelf wine. Then there was the usual stream of cigarette smokers and nighttime revelers who would pit-stop for supplies before continuing to the beach.

On a weeknight, the stream of patrons staggered to a trickle around eight. The young clerk grabbed his studies from beneath the counter and started reading that day's lessons. When the door chimed, he looked up and noticed some graduate students entering. Practically unnoticed was a hooded stranger that walked in behind them. The stranger slithered through the store while the grad students argued over what wine to pick.

With bottles in hand, the students paid and left as the hooded stranger coiled by the candy rack. When the door clanged behind the students, the stranger came to the cash register and threw down some Wrigley's gum and a chocolate bar.

The young clerk mentally added the total and said, "That'll be fifty-five cents."

For the first time since he entered the store, the stranger's face came into view. Simultaneously, the stranger effortlessly pulled a gun from under his hooded sweatshirt. The weapon coiled before the young clerk, black, like the pits on a viper.

"Give me all the money," the stranger's gun said.

For both young men, time slowed down.

The seconds seemed endless to the clerk who could count the scratches on the gun's barrel but would not look into his tormentors' eyes for fear of what he would see.

The seconds were endless for the gun-wielding young man who felt each moment as a moment closer to capture.

Clerk – Gun – Stranger. Stranger – Gun – Clerk.

The clerk was shoveling bills into a brown paper bag.

"Faster," was all that the stranger's gun said.

Once the cash register was empty and the clerk started to hand his tormentor the money, he thought about the alarm under the counter, but before he could decide, the hooded stranger directed him to lie face down behind the counter.

Once he was face down, the clerk could hear nothing but the pounding of his own heart, THUMP, THUMP, and with each beat came the vision of his lifeless body in grainy black and white police photos. THUMP, THUMP, THUMP, a chalk line shrine would be all that remained of him. THUMP, THUMP, THUMP, THUMP.

Above him, the hooded stranger paused and thought to himself, use a gun, go to prison.

THUMP, THUMP, THUMP, THUMP, THUMP.

He knew my face...

THUMP, THUMP.........CLICK!!!

They say that you never hear the shot that kills you.

At eight twenty-six p.m. on November sixteenth, 1978, two men met for the last time.

I heard the wind whistling through the branches, or was it someone weeping?

I knew both of those men.

Death Abides

Your fate abides,
but you gotta go around the next corner to find her.

Lying like a fetus in the feted womb of a wet alleyway, you struggle, but you cannot move. You feel the goosebumps bloom on your arm. Your breath bubbles the dank puddle, which covers the right side of your head. Your unsubmerged eye focuses upon some clattering movement from behind the grease encrusted dumpster. You can barely discern the clumsy, black, nightmare cat as it crawls toward you.

Its visage, the crooked countenance of roadkill. Its legs have been replaced with roughhewn, wooden stakes that click-clack as it approaches your face.

Your mind screams at your body to move. No response.

The tiny beast's one right eye dilates to capture the darkness of the alleyway, the other eye hangs at the end of its ocular cord and sways like a rubbery mace as its sharp legs clatter forward. The detached eye sways on its tenuous tether; it emits a sickening yellow light that appears to curdle reality. As it casts its pallor, reality's sharp edges spoil like rotting meat.

Your will screams through every fiber of your being, move.

Move. Move god damn it, MOVE.

Your body cannot respond as this dripping beast pierces the veil that separates aspirational dreams from cold sweat nightmares. The creature rips through your reality like the blood-curdling scream of a sudden knife strike.

Death's feted aroma fills your mouth as you gulp in each bubbling breath.

Then the tiny beast scraps your hand with it coagulated black fur. It begins to walk down the length of your arm. Each of its jagged wooden legs stabs your arm, leaving a pumping wound.

Your eye strains to look up, and you see the scattered moonlight reflect off the tiny beast's needle teeth. As it opens its maw, a retching smell overcomes you in a narcotic wave. You vomit into the puddle that cradles your face. The tiny beast is now atop your head with its piercing legs finding balance in your neck and forehead. It crouches down and begins to lick your face. With repeated licks, it feasts on your derma. You hear it purr with satisfaction.

Its raspy tongue laps and feeds. Your prayers are not for escape; they are now prayers for release. You pray for a merciful end. You have given up on living and enjoin death to take you.

To make it all go away.

But death has no ears. Death has no eyes. Death cannot speak. Death only reaps.

I startle awake from my bedside vigil. My dad's withered body lays in a fetal position underneath his sheets. Each of his breaths gurgles since they removed the machines and the tubes from his arms. And we wait — he within his dreams and me within this nightmare. And neither of us can will our bodies to move.

As Death abides.

CHAPTER 4:

FAITH

Only fools and saints dare to put themselves in harm's way and expect to come out unscathed. I'm no saint; I'm more akin to a lucky jerk. Even a fool has faith. Fools trust that leaping and then looking will turn out for the best. Now that is faith. A belief that I am tapping into more and more. You see, every new venture contains a level of risk, a level of the unknown, and it takes faith to jump anyway.

Options

You define your character by your choices
when only bad choices remain.

O nce you have taken the jump, you've left most of your options behind.

In La Jolla Cove, where the Pacific Ocean crashes into the rough-hewn cliffs, there is a secret place hidden in a clef atop those cliffs. It's called the Clam. Like nature's diving board, it is a smooth rock that is suspended thirty feet above the translucent green crashing sea.

Peering down from the Clam, you'll see the subterranean flora sway to the rhythm of surging waves. Look too long, and you'll become hypnotized by its metronomic motion and may lose your balance, not a good thing with only the cold water to catch you.

The Clam was a secret spot that only locals knew about, although an adventurous visitor or two might stumble upon it. It was here that you would dive into an exhilarating mixture of rushing wind and bracing water. The inertia of your thirty-foot dive would send your body down, ten feet or more, beneath the waves. Swimming up from your plunge, you'd open your eyes into the emerald liquid world of rocky terrain and swaying plants. Breaking the surface, you'd scream back to your friends in shouts filled with the combination of rush and relief. Relief? Yes, relief. Each dive must be in sync with the surge of the ocean. As the wave hits the cliffs, the depth of the sea swells to an acceptable depth of twenty feet. Time your jump incorrectly, and you had the real possibility of diving into the submerged rocks.

Now, as a rule, diving into rocks of any kind was to be avoided. Then again, looming danger was the bearnaise sauce to this experience. Without risk, why dive at all? Well, that's a question you'd ask if you were young and foolish.

But when there was an audience of tourists, our lower-case foolishness rose to FOOLISHNESS in all caps. On one such day, a group of German tourists had hiked to the Clam as we were diving. These tourists walked cautiously to the cliff's edge and peered down into the depths below. They jostled and chided each other in a language none of us knew. They watched us stand on the precipice of the Clam and carefully timing the surge; we would arc into the air and then crash into the water below. We had learned to interlock our fingers to break the surface tension of the ocean, thus mitigating the inevitable crash on our heads. We were foolish, not stupid.

The tourists were amazed and entertained, but we had just gotten started. We decided to go full superhero. I don't know who thought of this first, maybe it was Bob, but the new plan was to get a running start. A blind start. One of us standing at the cliff's edge would shout, "surfs up," denoting that the swell was high. Then another one of us would run down the winding path, timing our run with the unseen next swell. With our towel tied around our necks (like a cape), we would start running down the twisted path that culminated at the Clam, where we would drop our towel/cloak and dive into the water.

Yeah, it was Bob that went first. At full gallop, he ran down the path. And with the precision of an actor, he dropped his towel/cape and arced into the ocean. The tourists ate this up. Then it came to my turn. What could I do to improve upon this foolishness? Why I'd do a front flip. I quickly formulated my procedure. I'd run at full speed down the path, drop my towel on the Clam and execute a forward flip, and hit the water.

As I took off, I had a nagging feeling that something was missing in my hasty calculation. As I launched into the air and began to execute my forward flip, the missing piece came to me.

Cary, what about the surge?

Cary, what about the lack of surge?

You see, I had started my run without hearing my friends letting me know if the surge was up or out.

Once you have taken the jump, you've left most of your options behind.

The arc of my dive offered me only moments of analysis.

Option one, I could complete my dive and hope, on the luck of my Irish heritage, that the surge was high, and everything would be OK.

Option two, I could finish my dive, and find out that the swell was low, and with the blessing of Murphy's Law, I could crack my thick Irish head on the submerged rocks.

Option three, is there an option three? Yes, yes, there was option three, but it was going to be a painful option. Option three was to finish my dive in a belly flop. Now a belly flop afforded me the luxury of a shallow entry regardless of the surge. But the thirty-foot fall would demand a Charon-like payment in pain for entry.

My mind raced.

Option one was just a hope.

Option two was a total nightmare.

Option three was a pain.

Gotta choose. Was it to be option one, option two, or option three?

I chose option three.

Mere milliseconds before I entered the water, I curled into a semi-fetal position and landed face and belly first into the cold Pacific.

SLAP!!

Surprisingly, it wasn't painful. Painful would imply that I had any feeling left in my face or my stomach. The resounding impact of the chilly Pacific had robbed me of any sensation.

After impact, I sunk like a leaf falling from a tree. As I sank deeper and deeper, the water became colder and colder, soothing the recovering nerve endings in my face and stomach. As I reached the end of my oxygen, I started swimming back up to the surface.

Once I broke through, I heard my friends and the tourists hooting and hollering in delight.

Bob shouted, "You Ok?"

All I could do was nod my head and start swimming back.

I hadn't broken anything but my pride. But on the upside, I had further cemented myself in the pantheon of stupid human tricks. I retired from diving for the remainder of that day.

Life, real life doesn't begin until you jump. It is during our falls that our lives are defined.

It takes a leap of faith (or folly) to start any worthwhile endeavor.

Trust yourself and JUMP!

The Wanderer

If you don't know where you are going,
every step becomes your final destination.

You crest the hill, and the morning sun momentarily blinds you to the vast mountain meadow that fills your horizon. The forest of hemlock and white pines protect the swaying grasses of this valley. Beyond this meadow, distant granite peaks invite you. But there is no trail. And you must decide. Stay the course or?

You stride forward into waist-high grasses that tickle your legs with each step. Without a path, you wander toward the wonder that awaits just beyond that granite horizon.

Wandering allows you to absorb the undersea qualities of this meadow. Your boots crunch the dry lakebed from which the grasses grow. Occasionally you stumble or kick the unseen rocks that lay below the gold-green grasses.

There is a beauty that reveals itself as you wander. Your senses are on alert, and the world becomes your private cinemascope. Wandering allows no agendas or time restraints. The whole world presents itself, and you are receptive to its wonder.

The insects swirl with a faint buzz, the birds dart in silence, and the deer stand with unflinching stares as you create a path that not even random chance could conjure.

Wanderer is a moniker that I embrace as I wander through a life where chance possibilities are taken in stride. Each chance possibility cast before my aimless life is a challenge to do my best.

From an introverted childhood that tossed me from coast to coast, I learned how to enjoy the solitude powered by my shyness. I learned to discover the mysteries of the new lands where our family settled, from the forest and fauna of Virginia, to the suburbia of Long Beach, California, to the bug and reptile menagerie that is Florida, and the shrub and chaparral of San Diego. From these imposed travels, I learned to love the variety that one's life has to offer.

In school, I created games for everything. Pages and pages of math problems became a timed race. I personified numbers into unique characters. Reading became a launchpad for my boundless imagination. Learning about our solar system morphed into my fantastical playground. Any task that would dull one's senses only challenged me to create a way to make it a game. To make it fun, then to have fun.

A wanderer in the world of work, I would find a way to make that fun too. While doing the most menial of tasks as a warehouseman at Levitts, my mind would wander. My imagination would be engaged in the colorful stories from my workmates as I swept the entire warehouse. My workmates could never understand my smile as I cleaned. To them, I was the odd duck, yet in my mind, I was the wild duck.

Life was a recipe comprised of places, people, and events that created some exciting dishes.

On a dreary day in August, I found myself on the side of the Al-Can highway in Canada, attempting to wave down a good Samaritan as my car laid in a ditch. This unfortunate event would present an opportunity to be a bush-teacher for the Headstart program, working out of Anchorage, Alaska.

Back in San Diego, I learned that digging ditches affords you a great tan and the muscular demeanor of a Greek god. Working with my back taught me about the satisfaction of sweat, hard work, and the pleasures of an icy beer. It was the summer that convinced me to go back to college, with more gratitude and a better attitude.

Oh, all the places I have been with nary a map to guide me. I never plotted a path for my life. My life has just been an open meadow of possibilities.

With childlike wonder, I keep cranking the jack-in-the-box of life. And life has never disappointed.

My wanderlust is fueled by gratitude and powered by faith that each doorway is a gateway.

Life is not a binary choice between the well-worn path and the path less taken. There is a third choice — to create a new path of your own. To look towards the virgin meadow of possibilities and see where that can take you.

Darwin's Pool

*If the lifeguard of life tells you to get out of the gene pool,
then it's not a good day.*

Motorcycles are a Darwinian device to purge the gene pool of fools.

If Darwin had could have been asked about motorcycles, I am sure that he would have said, "It's all fun and games until someone gets hurt, then it's hilarious!"

At seventeen, I did not have enough common sense to purchase Darwin's book, but I did have enough cash to buy my first dirt bike.

Imagine my surprise when:

There I was, soaring high into the azure blue desert sky astride my roaring dirt bike, suspended by nothing more than youthful invincibility and stupidity. And it was the stupidity I was banking on because only dumb luck would extricate me from my ten-story arc of doom.

When your life hangs in the balance, your mind gains clarity. Time slows way down, and your mind quickens. Random thoughts stream through your mind. I remember looking down and seeing my six friends. I thought, what an auspicious number — the exact amount needed for pallbearers.

I was sure that my pallbearers, I mean my friends, were divining my chances of survival as somewhere between a snowball's chance in hell, and chastity at Woodstock.

As I was flying high, I wondered, would they be serving nuts on this flight. Nuts???? Yes, because when you have a raging 250cc motorcycle between your legs and you are suspended ten stories above the desert floor, knowing the precise location of your nuts is of utmost importance.

It was right about then that I began my descent.

Now there are two things you must remember if you find yourself hurtling down a mountain on a dirt bike:

Number One: You must remind yourself not to use the front brake. Failure to heed this warning will result in a whirling cartwheel that would make a seasoned Cirque du Soleil performer puke and cry.

Number Two: You must ensure that the motorcycle lands on both tires at once. You see, the launch sets you off with the front tire above the back, and that hill is sloping away from you. So, against all bastions of common sense, you must willfully point the nose of the bike down. To accomplish this step, you slide yourself off of the foam seat and straddle the metal gas tank to correct the angle of the motorcycle. And as you straddle the metal gas tank, again ask, "Flight attendant, Flight attendant, where are my nuts?"

As the point of impact nears, things happen in hyper speed. Thoughts and actions meld.

Impact in three...two...one...bammb!!!

"Ahh...Never mind, I found my nuts."

You slam on the back brake as hard as you can, although, in the sand, it offers little resistance.

Then you come off the dune and on to the dried sand bed, but your ride is not over. You see the shallow ravine approaching and know that you must lay down the bike. The hardpan ground covered by blown sand provides an unexpectedly slippery surface, and the bike comes down on top of your leg.

Now skidding on your side toward the ravine, you catch a whiff of barbecue. No, not the aroma of southern barbecue, more like zombie come to dinner barbecue as your bike's hot exhaust pipe burns through your motorcycle leathers, but no time to worry you fly over the edge of the ravine and slam into its far wall.

You come to a full and complete stop. From dizzying heights to lying in a ditch, your ride is done.

You slowly stand up and dust yourself off. Looking down, you see your dirt bike partially buried into the ravine. You smell the burnt hairs from your leg that will never grow back. From deep inside you, a smile cracks the dust on your face, and the rush becomes whole.

You have survived to swim another day in the gene pool. You turn to your friends and shout, "Who's next!!"

Because it's true, it is all fun and games until someone gets hurt, then it's hilarious.

CHAPTER 5:

AWARENESS

Let the world pour into every one of your five senses. Then see as if your eyes had never been open. Then hear like a baby listening to its mother's voice for the first time. Then touch like the tenderness of that first kiss. Then smell like a beggar outside a bakery. Then taste like you just stole a finger full of icing. Feel the rush of your senses. Inhale health, wealth, and happiness. Pause. Exhale peace, love, and gratitude. Answers reside within everything because every little thing is an integral part of all things. Connect to anything, and you immediately connect to the universe.

A Nerd, a Stoner, and a Prom Queen

Can't sing the lyrics if you can't hear the song

Being part of a team is like being in a caldron for growth. As teammates, we learn the miracle of one multiplied by us. If the feeling moves us, we can learn to lead and share what only teammates can know. There is a third, hidden feature; that is learning the art of listening and learning from those who surround us.

My epiphany about teamwork came when I was a freshman in high school. I was taking summer school biology at Patrick Henry High. On my first day of class, I learned that everyone else was there to make-up biology. I was the lone freshman in a class full of juniors, a sheep among wolves. Besides the age difference, there was also an experience gap.

When the teacher handed out the syllabus, I remember thinking how cool it would be to dissect all these creatures and do genetic experiments. Biology class and the word fun were not the prevailing mindsets of others in this class. Most considered summer school biology as doing time. Their past failures confined them.

Outside of the obvious physical clues: my stature, lack of facial hair, and bookworm demeanor, it was easy to peg me as a nerd. I was a nerd. I was a nerd when it was uncool to be a nerd. Oh, and I was the worst type of nerd — the type of nerd who loved being a nerd. So, you can imagine my surprise at how many other students wanted me on their team; I was surprised, flattered, and a bit puzzled.

54

I ended up on a team with two other students, Bill and Michelle. Bill was a classic Fast Times at Ridgemont High stoner with long, sun-bleached hair and a scraggly beard. (Oh my God, I just described Shaggy from Scooby-Doo.) Bill was a funny guy. For Bill, life as a stoner was an endless series of hilarious misadventures. Or was that just the pot is talking?

Then there was Michelle. She was as tall as Bill, and she had the entire package, as they say. Bill confided in me that Michelle was one of the popular girls at Patrick Henry High and was on tract to become next years prom queen.

Now when it came to doing the biology experiments, we were down to two, just Michelle and me. Bill would always be looking out the window or engaged in pratfalls off the high lab stools.

To tell you the truth, Michelle was as superficial with her studies as (I assume), she was within her social circle. It was often just down to me. I held no resentment because, as I worked the experiments, my teammates were teaching me about a world I had never known.

Bill regaled me with his smoking exploits and his narrow misses with the long arm of the law, while Michelle gave me glimpses of her social life, the parties, the outings, and how she played the field.

Every morning that summer, I woke up excited to go to class. For me, it was like taking a double major, I was learning biology, and with the help of Bill and Michelle, I was learning about life.

When that class was over, I got my grade and a free pass to take chemistry in the fall. More importantly, I learned firsthand about the hilarity of a stoner's life. I learned about the insecurities of a beautiful girl and her stress to stay relevant. And I learned there was an abundant life that existed outside the pages of books.

That experience taught me much more than biology. It taught me how to follow, then to lead, and to always listen.

Life is a long song. Each of us has our chorus to sing.

And if we listen very hard, we can learn from those around us the lyrics of life and sing along.

Roadside

Death is a lesson for the living

When I was young, I saw the carcass of a black cat that had been killed by racing traffic and tossed to the side of the road. The painful emotions that racked my immature mind and body from that vision reoccurred every day as I passed that spot on my way to school. I was horrified by my fascination, yet my imagination raced to reenact the last frantic moments of that cat's ninth life. I could not cope with such a gruesome sight, so I started to look away. I did not want to see the bad. With simple logic, I theorized that if I didn't look, it wouldn't be there. And in that sense, the dead cat disappeared. The ugly part of life could just be wished away into the cornfields of the Twilight Zone.

As my glass-half-full life continued into high school, I became comfortable with the childhood magic of looking away. Then one Monday in January of my sophomore year, I learned that Neil had died.

Neil and I were school buds. We had eaten lunch together every day since freshman year. School news, new music, new books, and what was happening next weekend were the topics of discussion. Neil was on the cheer squad and a manager for the junior varsity football team. And at St. Augustine High school, football was everything. Neil was an athletic guy with no specific discipline. We were on the same flag football intermural team and played against each other on the intermural basketball teams. Neil lived a walking distance from campus, and we often hung out at his house after school.

One Saturday night, Neil was the sole passenger in his older brother's car. Speed and a slick corner caused the small vehicle to slam into a light pole. Neil had been crushed to death as the streetlight flickered out.

His death shattered my glass-half-full life. In my grief, my imagination could not control the urge to relive the last moments of Neil's life.

I imagined Neil's body coursing with the thrill of speed. Then momentarily filled by the indigestible poison of fear as the car began to skid. The squeal of tires followed by the thundering reverberation of an impact, an impact that would crush him, his family, and his surviving brother.

At Neil's funeral, much of my school turned out, football players, other school athletes, and his closest friends. Flowers, pictures, and tears filled the church, yet my mind kept flashing back to the image of that dead cat on the side of the road. That horror that had fascinated me so long ago flowed into the horror that I experienced after Neil's death. Standing in that church, I forced myself to look deeply into the shattered soul of Neil's brother. I looked deeply into the lives Neil had affected and deeply into my grief. I got up from the church pew and walked up to his casket. I looked down at Neil in his final repose. As I stared down at him, I saw for the first time the lifeless eyes of that dead cat and realized how much of my life I had excluded.

That visceral experience of death and love broke my blindness.

With that pain and joy swirling within me, I vowed never to look away again. Never to be reluctant to make lasting connections. Never to wish-away into the cornfields of my mind anything that I did not want to see or feel.

Look deeply, feel deeply, and never look away. Life has brought you an opportunity, learn everything you can about it because everything you experience will be on your final exam.

Postcards from Alaska

Look for what lies beneath

Think Alaska, think cold. It is cold, the kind of cold that permeates your bones. But it's not the cold, it is the prolonged winter nights that wear you down. Locals call it cabin fever. Those four walls that protect you feel like they are closing in around you. You are a prisoner in a land of twilight and night.

Like every prisoner, you dream of an escape from your isolation. Yet in those few, precious hours of daylight, when you open your living room shades, all you can see are rolling hills of deep snow that resemble a frozen ocean. Will you forsake the relative comfort of your prison to venture into the vast, frozen whiteness?

I carefully opened the front door. Like sniffing a fine red wine, I sipped the air through my nose to judge just how cold it was. If the cold, dry air only slightly burnt the hairs in my nostrils, I would stride out into the white.

In a land of virgin snow, where your every step is like a footfall on the moon, I walked and walked until I burst out from beneath the trees to a shoreline of frozen, white waves, stretching out before me. Upon this border, I paused to turn up my collar and muster my resolve to venture out from the trees. At that moment, I looked back.

There, at the feet of the last circle of trees, bits of black loam, deep green and vibrant red lichen, lay scattered over the white winter canvas. A rabbit had exited its warm wintery burrow and created this minimalistic painting — a painting signed by the artist's tracks, which faded off into the distance.

My eyes explored the cozy darkness of the vacated burrow. A hobbit-home splotched with leafy greens and wooden browns that fade into interesting obscurity.

As I turned again to look out over the snowbound vista, my feeling of isolation dissipated and, in its place, grew the realization that beneath the snow lies burrows of unexplored warmth and richness.

Whether you are trudging through the snows in the Alaskan wilderness, or walking the crowded streets of New York, or lost in a Black Friday shopping crowd of humanity, that feeling of isolation can wash over you in an instant. When this occurs, take a moment to investigate the world that exists beneath your gaze.

One Black Friday, steps from the double doors of Sam's Club, a signature gatherer approached me. She rattled on about the ballot initiative that she was collecting signatures.

As I scribbled my name, I asked, "How was your Thanksgiving?"

She started slowly talking about her day with family. I chimed in that our relatives cooked so ours couldn't have been better. The more I shared about my day with my family, the more she began to share about hers. She shared how the aroma of the twenty-pound turkey filled her home — detailed the dinner table filled with every side dish imaginable topped off with three sweet potato pies for dessert. She smiled as she revisited the gathering. Then she paused and, in a halting voice, talked about her son, who for another year did not attend. I felt her parental pain of an errant son. I paused, then began to share how I had been that son. And how my mother's love and patience allowed me to ultimately reconnect. We shared our pain. We shared our human connection.

Beneath the self-imposed isolation, we had discovered our humanity that lay dormant underneath the Black Friday rush. Like finding a warm burrow beneath that cold blanket of Alaskan snow.

What lies beneath?

We lie beneath.

Share yourself, and you'll discover a rich world buried just beneath the visible.

The Reason for Pain

Thank you, sir, may I have another

Beneath the towering canopy of an ancient Japanese forest, a Zen monk hiked across the rugged terrain strewn with moss-covered rocks and decaying, fallen trees. Anxious to arrive at his destination, he quickened his pace. His haste became a slip, and he thudded to the ground. Protruding from his calf was a blood-covered bone. Pain threatened to suffocate his consciousness. He calmed his breathing. Gently, he put his hands together, and raised them in front of his face, positioned his index fingers on his forehead, and applied pressure.

The longer he did this, the more bearable his pain became. In concentrating on that pain, he diminished it.

Each of us has that point on our bodies. Mine is on the underside of my wrist. Whenever something happens, I apply pressure to my wrist, which allows me to focus my attention and dissipate my pain. It works for me every time, but I might have a little help from genetics.

My grandfather on the Cook side of the family was a man of short stature who held some fine and fertile farmland. During harvest season, he required the assistance of roustabouts. One season he hired three roustabouts who one day decided that working for wages was too hard, and it would be easier to take. They started pummeling my grandfather. But he would not give an inch. One blow broke my grandfather's nose, and another cracked a rib. As he received, so did he deliver, his calloused hands and his vice-like grip tore into these foes. Bleeding, bruised, and battered, my grandfather stood as these men began to tire and cower. The roustabouts started to realize that short of killing my grandfather, they could not win. They took off.

His stand your ground attitude earned him much respect in the back hills of Indiana. Most folks wondered how he could have lasted so long in a fight where he received three blows to everyone he landed. A mystery answered by my youngest brother — an answer written in his blood.

Our family had just moved back to California, and we were renting an old nineteen-fifties home. Three tall steps lead to the back door. In a rush, Dave tripped on the first step and crashed headlong on to the edge of the second step. But not a whimper or a cry was heard, even by my mom, who was working in the kitchen just above the back doorstep. It was only by serendipity that she walked out of the back door, and aghast with horror witnessed her three-year-old son mopping up pools of his blood on the back steps — not wanting to be scolded for the mess that his head wound had made.

Well, as it turned out, Dave has a high tolerance for pain. As a matter of safety, my mom would send him out to play in a football helmet. But that did not prevent Dave from breaking bones. Once, a neighbor accidentally slammed Dave's foot in a garage door, breaking it. Dave just hobbled around and continued to play until it was time to go home for supper.

As an adult, Dave was out in Glamis, riding his three-wheeled all-terrain-cycle over the dunes. After one jump, he crashed, yet as he was picking up his three-wheeler, another rider soared over that same hill pinning Dave's leg against his trike. That rider did not stop to help; he just drove off, leaving Dave crippled. Dave had to reach down and wrench his leg back the ninety degrees to reset his leg correctly. He remounted his machine and rode back to his solitary camp.

Once at camp, he didn't reach for the first aid kit, nope, he reached for the cooler and downed a couple of ice-cold beers. Then he crawled into the bed of his truck and fell asleep. The next day he drove a hundred miles plus journey back home to San Diego.

Once home, the news was grim. The initial prognosis was that Dave may not ever use that leg again, let alone go back to his higher-wire, ironworker's job. By sheer good luck, when it was time to get a second opinion, the orthopedic surgeon for the San Diego Clippers was still in town and he agreed to take the case.

After the surgery, it was off to physical therapy. The medical team told Dave that it would be nine months before he could return for work. But Dave's high tolerance for pain proved that estimate wrong again. In three months, he was back on skyscrapers, doing his job.

And you know what, there is a little bit of my grandfather's high tolerance for pain in me too. Growing up, friends were constantly reminding me that my leg was bleeding down into my shoe or that I had a goose-egg on my forehead from that last hit. Now my tolerance for pain was nothing like my brother's and nothing like my grandfather's, but it still resided there inside me.

Yep, I had a high tolerance for pain until I reached puberty. That's when I meet, Devon. First love, puppy love, or true love — who could tell. Devon was my best friend's younger sister. She was the love of my life. When I was around her, I could feel my heart beating. Thump, thump. Thump, thump. My heart raced. I was full of energy. Thump, thump, thump, thump.

When I learned that I was not the love of her life, it was like my heart stopped beating.

Her rejection tore my heart out of my chest, then threw it into rushing traffic. It was the first time that I experienced real pain. To dissipate this pain, I frantically pressed the underside of my wrist, but it did not work. Not at all. I was utterly devastated. It was such a bitter sensation that I thought that my best course of action would be NOT to fall in love again. Not then, not the next day, not ever.

Thank god that love is more persistent than I am stubborn.

And when I did learn to love again, I discovered that those two extremes, having a high tolerance for physical pain and a low tolerance for emotional distress, taught me that life is a spectrum. And that pain is a part of that rainbow. If you miss the pain, you'll miss life's full experience. The pain that I felt then allows me to tap into gratitude for love now.

Within the gnarled growth of briar, lie the sweetest berries that few dare to taste.

Dark, Thin Silhouette

Who can decide when both sinners and saints are so appealing?

I was in love. All I could think about was being in her company. Spending time together and remembering all the individual episodes we shared felt like mainlining euphoria.

But then that sinister, dark silhouette of deceit, followed by lies, and then betrayal crept in and crushed my heart.

When you are in that much emotional pain, what do you do? Do you talk to your friends? Do you go to some secluded spot and work it out alone? Nope, you go to some dimly lit bar and get plastered.

That is how I found myself in an unsteady stagger, getting into my car. The alcohol had only inflamed my anger over the lies and deceit. I keep mulling it over — had she ever told me the truth, was anything I heard from her real. I slammed my foot to the accelerator.

When I arrived home, my mind was still swirling in a cocktail of rage and alcohol. I did not go in; I went to the garage. I found my toolbox. I picked up a hammer, no, not that one. I then picked up the large framing hammer. I began to swing it, feeling its weight in my hand.

With that hammer in hand, I stole quietly into my house. I hid the framing hammer behind my back. I nonchalantly sallied up to my slim, black beauty. So thin, so elegant.

Down came that hammer, powered by hate and rage. I swung again and again until all that remained were the splattered remains of my flat-screen TV.

That's right; I killed my flat-screen. I must say it was liberating.

After liberating myself from her manipulation, I finally answered the question of who is the puppet and who is the puppet-master.

Sure, sure, you may be your own man. You may be a confident woman. But how sure can you be that you are not just an amalgam created by a sleepless foe that feeds you information about what you should think and how you should feel?

During those moments, when we think we are relaxing, the networks infiltrate our unconscious minds. Whether we are laughing or crying, it's because we have been consuming an unlabeled product.

During the nineteen-sixties, television pressured women to be the perfect homemaker in the guise of Donna Reed and Barbara Billingsley. During the seventies, it was the faux hippie rebellion of the Mod Squad. In the nineties, we depreciated fatherhood with the likes of Homer Simpson and Al Bundy in Married with Children. And tonight, when you turn on your favorite show, you will see a cast of beautiful people. They are a reality that we can never match. So, we are sold products to fill that void.

And the nightly news, WHOOP, do not get me started. It is not that the nightly news is telling lies, oh no, they are more intelligent than that; it is what they focus and don't focus on that pulls our strings.

Ask yourself, who is the puppet, and who is its master?

I do not see some conspiratorial triumvirate hiding in the dark shadows. Yet when we turn off our critical thinking and just veg out on our sofa, we must ask ourselves, are those network cables or are they the puppet master's strings?

Of course, our lives can be enhanced, enriched, and embellished by what we see and hear. Think of all the great movies that awaken in you new questions, new perspectives, and personal insight that otherwise would have been untapped or unexplored.

We all love network feed, but there are strings attached.

See those strings and fall freely in love again with that siren we call television.

CHAPTER 6:

INTEGRITY

O ur only purpose in life is to find out who we are and then become the best we can be —a simple two-step process, self-discovery, and self-actualization.

Simple but not easy.

Life, like a cryptic cipher, leaves clues in the most innocuous places, like a sewer or the soul of a cat. Since life moves at the speed of thought, those crucial clues are like dandelion seeds in a whirlwind. Catch them, and the lessons will be profound. The seeds of genius within Leonardo da Vinci sprouted during his long walks and simple observations. In silence, he'd walk, watch, and wonder, and during these quiet times, the universe would lay itself bare at his feet. A good friend of mine said that all his answers to life's problems came to him as he showered. Another friend resolved many of her gnawing issues while she gardened. A mind, otherwise engaged, is like a magic key to the most persistent problems.

Along our sojourn in this life, we encounter a plethora of waystations that allow us to refuel and refresh ourselves. It is these moments of respite that our true selves are most accessible.

Play Your Hand

My Dad would tell me,
"Cary, in life, you gotta play the cards that are dealt ya."

Yet if you look up from the table of life and see that fickle Fate is your dealer, then you gotta expect that the hand you're dealt just might stink. And this is the story of one of those hands.

One year before the United States bicentennial, I found myself hitchhiking back to San Diego from Anchorage, Alaska with just a backpack, a straw hat, a smile on my face, and a degree in early childhood development in my pocket.

"Come on, man, give me a ride."

"Hey, buddy, you got plenty of room. I'll throw my backpack between your chain saws and those hockey masks."

"You going south, then you're going my way."

Once I arrived in San Diego, I quickly discovered that my early childhood development degree was worth — what's the technical term, ah yes, diddly squat. It was economically unviable. A good friend said he could get me a job in construction.

"Cary, dude, you'll be working outside in San Diego, no dress code, tan bodies, best shape of your life, and the pay is good."

I said, "Sign me up!"

What he did not tell me was that the job entailed installing sewer lines.

Truth be told, most of the time, installing sewer lines is a snap. Just digging a ditch and making damn sure that the pipes always flow downhill. Why? Because, as it says in the Good book (chapter and verse) of St. Peter the Plumber, "crap floweth downhillith."

As a matter of fact, the company that I worked for liked that motto so much that they emblazoned it on the side of all their trucks. In keeping with that motto, I, being the newest member of the team, was volunteered to connect our sparkling new sewer line to the old, live sewer line. (Live in sewer nomenclature means, "You would rather be dead then go near a live sewer line".)

There I was in a very old part of San Diego just north of the Del Mar Racetrack when I cracked open that manhole cover and was greeted by ghosts. The ghost of dinners past. The smell was strong enough to make a grown man cry, and a young man run for the hills.

Then it was time for me to go down into that manhole. Each rung was encrusted and rusted, but they held my weight. Down, down, down I went until I reached the bottom. I hung my lantern on one of the rusted rungs and turned it on.

What I witnessed next was nothing short of a life-altering lesson.

New manholes are composed of pre-formed concrete rings that are as smooth as a baby's bottom. Each ring is stacked one upon another until you reach the road level, then you pop on a manhole cover. Voila, you are done.

What I discovered when I turned on my lantern was a manhole wholly built by hand. Brick by brick by brick by brick. What craftsmanship! I said craftsmanship, not crapmanship.

Each brick was meticulously placed, no brick was askew, there was no extra mortar. This cylindrical structure was a work of art. This was the Sistine Chapel of manholes. That's when I started to think about the craftsman who created this masterpiece. Some seventy years before, this man placed each brick with all his skill, knowing that upon

71

completion, his masterpiece would be buried and forgotten. This manhole was to become my standard of integrity forever.

Like that craftsman, every brick we place in the manhole of our life is a reflection of us.

Everything that we do, everything we say, everything we write, and everything we make is us. It is a piece of us. This elegant manhole reminded me never to give less than what is possible, regardless of the situation, place, or time.

About that time, my boss yelled down, "Cary, get your butt in gear, you got three more of these to do this morning."

Fate had dealt me another stinkin' hand.

And yet, if you play your cards right, you might discover the secret to life, even in a sewer.

Moonshadow

At Christmastime, it's not how beautiful the box is; it's what's inside that make the child smile.

Don't you hate waking up before the alarm goes off? It's like living some Stockholm syndrome sitcom.

"Thank you, sir, may I have another?"

It's like a dog that salivates before the bell. What would Pavlov think about that?

It happens to me all the time. I find myself shuffling through the darkness to the bathroom, turning on the light, and staring into that face in the mirror and saying, "This just won't do!"

I am not the greying man in the mirror; I am a vibrant soul on an endless trek — a trek towards an infinite horizon.

I am not who I see; I am who I believe.

We are not who we see; we are who we believe!

That is the lesson I learned from the most unlikely of teachers.

This sage never wrote a bestseller, never presented on stage in front of thousands, heck this teacher never even spoke a word that I could understand. This guru of enlightenment was a cat. Yes, a cat. By the way...

I hated cats!

Those arrogant, little balls of fur that eat your food, scratch your furniture (and your friends), and then won't deign to give you the time of day. Did you ever try to call a cat? They'll look at you, put their little noses in the air, and then flip you off with their tails as they walk away.

I hated cats!

I hated cats so much that I went so far as to craft a tiny little sign that appears on the bottom of our front door. The calligraphic note states:

"Cats not Allowed!! ... That means you, you arrogant little bastards!"

Yep, I hated cats, until that one, rainy night when my wife came through the door with a petite, brindled bundle of fur.

She explained that as she exited the supermarket, she heard a soft, barely audible plea, "meeoooz, meeooz," coming from a rain-soaked cardboard box.

There inside, she found one, lonely, little kitten. The kitten had burrowed herself under the newspaper that lined the rapidly saturating cardboard box. Marge picked her up and felt the chill in her little paws. Without pause, she walked to the car and put the tiny bundle in her scarf-lined console unit.

On the rainy ride home, amongst the shards of moonlight, she named the sleeping bundle Moonshadow — an inspired moniker for the tortoiseshell-colored kitten.

When she arrived home, I proclaimed that although her generosity was laudable, it was a cat. Then I directed my wife to review Cary's Law for Cats:

Statement #1: Cary hates cats.

Statement #2: Kittens are cats.

Therefore: Cary hates kittens.

I went back to my computer to work while she tended to Moonshadow.

Regardless of all her attention, grooming, and preening, Marge could not get Moonshadow to stop meowing. In desperation, she cracked open my office door and pleaded with me to take Moonshadow while she took a break.

"Are you kidding? You know how much I hate cats and kittens!"

I again reminded her of Cary's Law for Cats.

"Please! She won't stop crying. I need a break. Please, honey, you know how animals love you."

"Animals, yes. Cats, never!"

"Please."

After endless protestation, I took the kitten, who immediately climbed up my tee-shirt, settled on my chest, and began kneading me with her sewing needle claws. After a mercifully short while, she slowly and clumsily climbed to the nape of my neck.

I could feel her racing heartbeat against my neck, then, oh so gradually, it slowed into a sleeping rhythm. There I sat, with this Moonshadow hanging over me as I went back to work on the computer.

As the days passed, I did my best to ignore the new kitten, knowing that a cat is always a cat, and I hated cats.

Then one day, while reading a book in bed, Moonshadow bounded up next to me and dropped a well-chewed tiny piece of trash next to my leg. She looked down at the wadded-up piece of paper, then up at me, then down at the wad, then up at me. Then down at the tiny trash ball, then back up at me.

Perturbed, I threw her trash ball towards the trashcan. As quick as thought, Moonshadow bounded after it. Retrieving it, she returned and dropped it again next to my leg. She looked down at the trash ball and then up at me. Then down at the ball, then back up at me.

I was more puzzled than before, so I took the ball of trash and flicked it to the other end of the room. She instantly flew as only a kitten can fly and caught the trash ball in mid-flight.

Now the game was on. I would flick it low, then flick it high, regardless of where it landed, Moonshadow would ferret it out and bring it back. The game continued until the kitten lay panting by my leg. Within moments she was asleep.

As she slept, I put my book down and started to ponder. Moonshadow was born a tiny kitten but instilled with a dog's spirit. A retriever to be precise.

I began to take an interest in this cat. A game of fetch was always the start. As soon as I got home and sat down, Moonshadow would find some small object, bring it to my chair, and we would repeat the now-familiar routine. She would look down at the toy then up at me, then down at the toy, then up at me.

That is when I began to think:

I am not who I see; I am who I believe.

We are not who we see; we are who we believe.

We are not who others see; we are who we believe!

Looking back over my life, I could see many examples of the truth that Moonshadow taught me.

I once met a beautiful woman who believed she was fatally flawed. As beauty is in the eye of the beholder, she could never see the truth that others saw. For her, that belief crippled her.

We are not who we see; we are who we believe.

At a 10k race in Chula Vista, I meet a paraplegic wheelchair participant who was not the lifeless legs that others saw. Legs that he carried around like an anchor. He was a restless spirit that could not wait to race.

He was not who others saw; he was the embodiment of his belief.

True Identity

Our junk mail defines us

The philosophical prowess of the Greeks created a massive body of literature that can be distilled down to two words:

Know thyself.

The pure power of these two words still resonates today. It resonates with each of us who search for our identity.

My childhood was a blur of travel.

By the time I was three, my family had moved six times. It wasn't until I was about six years old that I began to feel the loss of each move. I remember waving goodbye while my friends faded into the distance as we drove to a new home, a new coast. I never entirely understood why we had to leave.

In Jacksonville, Florida, my best friend lived just down the block. His name was Butch. Butch and I were the same age, and we both wore glasses, big black-framed glasses designed for men.

We were inseparable. We began to dress alike. We began to tell everyone that we were twins. It was a fanciful game, yet in hindsight, my assumed identity as Butch's twin might have foreshadowed something larger.

The ostensible reason for our peripatetic lifestyle was that my dad was in the navy. But was that the whole truth? Or was it just the cover story for a family under some governmental witness protection program?

Sheer foolishness, you say? Some tinfoil conspiracy. Well, consider these facts:

First, there was my dad, whose name was Archie. Yes, Archie, not short for Archibald or a cute moniker for Arch. It was Archie. Though his name was unusual, it was not something that would evoke further exploration. That was until we went to visit his hometown. When we came upon dad's neighbors, they all greet him as Bob. Bob, in no way or by any stretch of the imagination, can be gleaned from Archie. Strange, very strange, but it did not stop there.

My mom was Jean. For my entire life, she had been Jean Kellems, and yet when we went to her relatives, they all called her Lula. I mean Lula? What was going on here?

Yet even before these visits to my folks' ancestral homes, there had been clues. When my younger brother was born, his birth certificate labeled him, John Kellems. The moment he arrived home from the hospital, my older sisters and my dad called him Mike. It was explained to me by one of my older sisters that his middle name was Michael, and they all agreed that they would be calling him Mike. So, Mike it was.

How was a six-year-old to make sense of all this? My dad's name was Archie, yet all his family called him Bob. My mom's name was Jean, but her family called her Lula, and my younger brother's name was John, but we all called him Mike. One could only reason that my family was custom made for the witness protection program.

Then out of the blue, my next oldest sister decided to change her name from Joyce, her given name, to her middle name, Christine. (It took me decades to stop calling her Joyce and start calling her Christine.) What was going to happen next? Would I be forced to change to using my middle name, Thomas?

That left my oldest sister Linda, myself, Cary, and my youngest brother, David, as the only ones in the family using their real names. I began to ask myself why. What memo did we miss? What governmental directive did we forget when our family came under the jurisdiction of the witness protection program. I began to question the most basic premise of my own identity, my name. Was I Cary, or was I someone else masquerading as Cary?

I needed to determine my identity, my true identity, even if I was from a family of aliases. Was I even born with the name Cary or was that my alias? Further investigation was required. And sure enough, when I found my birth certificate, it was sketchy. On the original document was the name Carey. Then attached to this document was stapled an additional document with my name as Gary. A third document, held on by a paper clip, indicated the name I go by today, Cary.

How could anyone "know thyself," when one could not even get their name straight? Was I a deep, deep mole planted by some foreign power? Was I marked man, part of a marked family who always had to move to elude detection? Then if so, how was I supposed to get in contact with my handlers?

Then it hit me! They (whoever they are) had been trying to contact me for years through the mail. Or should I say, junk mail. All those mislabeled advertisements were actual communique from my mysterious government handlers. I started to sift thought the weekly piles of junk mail and discovered a curious pattern.

On Mondays, I would receive junk mail for Gary. On Wednesday, I would receive junk mail for Carey. On Saturdays, it was addressed to Thomas. But what could it mean? In the beginning, I visited the places that these mysterious mailers would mention. I went to get my car washed, got my nails done, and had every salesperson under the sun sell me a new roof, vinyl windows, chimney sweeps, and sewer washes. But no luck. No mysterious figure gave me my next orders.

What was I missing, what piece of the puzzle was I missing?

On Monday, after receiving my junk mail for Gary, I started cutting out words from each of those pieces of junk mail. On a whim, I cut out the first word of Monday's mail (for Gary). Then cut out the third word of Wednesday (Carey) mail, and on Saturday, I cut out the sixth word. I then pasted these words down and was astounded to see what it said.

Yes, although it looked like some serial killers' manifesto, it was the story of my life. To be precise, it was the story that I have just relayed to you, minus the punctuation.

I had been reading it all along. And I had been following orders.

Yes, I learned my identity by reading my junk mail. And to tell you the truth, it helped me feel whole, feel complete.

I love junk mail!

To this day, I never, ever, throw away any of my junk mail because without junk mail, how can one "know thyself"?

Tiny Green Army Men

The discovery of self is the start of the discovery of the universe

Ouse parties were BIG during the post-high school/pre-college days. They were colloquially known as keggers, yet drinking was never limited to just beer.

During these parties, every room had a purpose. Music, talk, and maybe some dancing filled the living and family rooms. The back patio was for the smokers (every type of smoker), and for those partygoers who needed a little fresh air. The bedrooms ... well use your imagination.

And then there was the kitchen. The kitchen was where you would find the beer keg and a mountain of the ubiquitous, red, plastic cups. Therefore, the kitchen was the one spot in the house that everyone visited at least once. They visited the kitchen if for no other reason than to confirm that they were at the right party. It was like touching the keg connected them to everyone at that party. Now without retribution, they could say, I was there.

The kitchen was where you would find me. I would be sitting on one of the countertops with my red cup of beer, a beer that would last me all night long. As people floated by, I would engage those I knew in conversation.

Most of the time, we would chit-chat, yet on occasion, our discussion would grow deep and heavy until someone else would saunter by, tell us to lighten up, and coax the passersby to rejoin the festivities in other parts of the house.

But I would stay. My spot in the kitchen afforded me the duality of being at the party but not "in" the party. From my perch, I could observe a world that fascinated me. I'd watch the parade of my peers. I studied what they wore and how they gathered. Who played with whom. It was a moving social puzzle that was visible when they thought no one was watching.

There would be groups of boisterous and animated guys. I would see the girls make their entrances, walking with poise, yet subtly nervous. I'd see the couples enter and scan the party for other couples. I was fascinated, but only interested in viewing it all from a distance. I never asked myself, "Why would I find this enjoyable?"

At the time, I wouldn't have been able to answer that question, but now I know why I preferred to be in the audience and not a player on the stage. That answer runs deep into my past.

As a navy brat, we moved often. Because of our peripatetic lifestyle, I was perennially the new kid in town. And if that weren't enough of an obstacle for a kid to overcome, I was also just plain shy. I often found myself playing alone in my room — playing with my little, green, army men. Or, in retrospect, should I say, my plastic, green, army therapists.

First, I would plot the battle plans on paper. I'd roughly sketch my room, the dresser, my bed, the window, and my desk. Then I'd overlay these sketches with troop placements, replete with artillery. I would strategize the installation of both the defensive and offensive positions. Once satisfied, I would dig my tiny, green troops out of my toy box.

I'd strategically place one set of troops on the high ground of my chest of drawers, the grenade throwers, and riflemen positioned on the very top. In one or two of the partially opened drawers, I would place my machine gunners and walkie-talkie guys. And after I had all the battlefield lines drawn and my plans of engagement scribbled down, I would take that piece of paper and fold it into an airplane. In the groove that ran the length of the plane, I put my general.

On the floor and up on my bed, I'd have the opposing forces — the underdog troops who had the impossible task of taking the high ground. And if I could find them in the colorful menagerie of my toy box, these troops would have artillery — small metal cannons and tanks.

I would then make many paper airplanes complete with hand-drawn insignia unique for each of the opposing sides.

Laying down on the floor with my troops and looking up at the edifice of the chest of drawers, I knew that this was going to be an uphill battle, but these men (these tiny, green, army men) had a can-do attitude.

Once I had all the troops in place, the battle would commence. The ground troops would make their move to capture the chest of drawers. As the battle lines clashed, I created a dialog and the sound effects:

"Ratta tat tat."

"Captain, I have been hit!"

"Boom, Crash...Boom!"

"They're tearing us to pieces! We need artillery support."

"Kasutt, crack, boom!"

"General, we've taken the first level."

And on and on. Until all the paper airplanes laid crumpled and the armaments capsized all over the floor.

These battles would go on for hours. Often my mom would peak inside to my room to ensure that the relative silence wasn't a reason to worry.

These little, green, army men did more than show courage, bravery, and sacrifice. They were a well-trained force that helped me deal with my shyness and my introverted nature. They taught me courage. They personified bravery. They helped me model how to work through obstacles and build perseverance. The perseverance that they demonstrated on my bedroom floor.

These little, green, army men helped me through all those tough times of adjusting to a new city and new friends. From them, I learned that solitude held infinite possibilities for enjoyment. That solitude recharged. That solitude was my library time to study each day's life lessons.

Reminiscing allows me to see my roots, to realize my true nature, my introverted life. I am an introvert in an extroverted world. And I'm OK with that.

These men of pressed, green plastic carried me over the troubled rivers of introversion. They allowed me to sharpen my intrapersonal skills and taught me to learn from each daunting new world that became our new home. They taught me that being an introvert was just an opportunity to see a wild world from a different perspective.

From my perch above the keg, I witnessed the passionate interactions of the party wildlife. What I learned, in measured doses, was how to connect with an always new, larger, more extroverted world, a world beyond the four walls of a lonely room.

We all search to find our place in this world. By serendipity, I found my way by following the path blazed by my tiny, green, army men.

Bright Eyes

Introverts don't necessarily dream of an extroverted world

The lights dim. A hush falls across the audience. Then the curtain rises.

The actors glimpse their audience. Hidden from their view, beyond the penumbra of the stage lights, a pair of bright eyes peer out. They are marveling at the fanciful freedom upon the stage. They feel a longing. Then tears of doubt fill these eyes.

The action of the actors on the stage beckons these two, bright eyes to play. But like the chains that burdened Marley to haunt Scrooge's dreams, those sparkling eyes remain fixed in the darkness. Iron chains forged by voices of false dogma.

"Children should be seen and not heard."

"Spare the rod and spoil the child."

"You can't do that; it'll take away from your scholastic achievement."

"So, you want to be a starving artist? What, are you stupid?"

Like Marley's chains, these rhythmic mantras of parental negativity and personal inadequacies bind bright-eyes to his chair. And in time, the curtain closes, and the actors leave.

In the back of the now dark theatre, those bright eyes close with the resounding thud of an iron door echoing down the corridor of a personal prison. Iron doubts hold the mind tight.

Within our solitude, we are clothed by loneliness and become lost in our thoughts. We decipher the world around us but cannot find the courage or motivation to step out of the shadows and stand under the bright, stage lights of life. The bright lights that are only matched by our own bright eyes.

My solitary confinement becomes a welcoming home, and the Stockholm syndrome is complete. Upon these dark prison walls, I paint windows to feint connection to the extroverted world.

On the periphery of the day-to-day world, you'll see the introverts at play. From our sanctuary in the shadows that surround the open grass, you might spy a bookworm lost between the lines. In books, we disengage from the day-to-day world into a world where we can play.

Living a life within versus living within life is the binary choice that many of us feel we must make. The dogma of either-or affixes to our introverted nature and we remain just a pair of bright eyes, look out from the boundaries of our minds.

Dispensing with this false dichotomy of an either-or life is my life's mission. Now I take the stage.

My bright eyes have learned so much about the world from the darkness of the audience. It is time to step out to the center of the stage. It starts with my acceptance that our lives, like great novels, arise from the eraser shavings of a thousand rewrites.

With these brave new steps, I discover the single, most significant tool of advancement ever created, the experience of failure. I mean, falling flat on my face, failure. And if I'm lucky enough, there will be an epic failure or two, which will catapult me toward my impossible goals.

Professor Murphy's adage;

"Anything that can go wrong, will go wrong," is my blessing and not my curse.

Through practice, with failure, I will rise from my seat and walk toward the stage, with my bright eyes ablaze.

CHAPTER 7:

INNER STRENGTH

Your trials and tribulations are necessary detours along the bumpy road of life. Like air, water, food, and shelter, difficulties and frustrations are the clay to form a new you. It is never the world that creates your weakness; it is your reaction to the world that reveals your strength. Walk proudly into the darkness, become energized by your terrors. Use this energy to swim out of the stagnate pool of self-pity. You'll discover your inner strength in the most innocuous situations. It may occur while you are staying alone in the darkness or under the lights of an arena.

My Last Redoubt

The storm above. Calm below.

The phone shatters my sleep. "Brring … Brring! … Brring!!!"

I turn over to answer it and squint to see the red numbers on my alarm clock read three thirty-three a.m. I pick up the call.

"Hello," I whisper, not trying to wake up Marge.

It's Bob on the other end. With an audible tone of panic in his voice, he says, "Cary, none of the dealership transmissions are getting processed. And the east coast goes live in less than two hours!"

Bordering on consciousness, I reply, "OK, Bob, I'll see you in about thirty minutes."

I hang up and get out of bed.

Marge, in her sleepy whisper, asks, "Who was that?"

"It was work, babe; I gotta go."

I walk to the bathroom to start my day. As I begin to shave, I think, "Does anything good ever comes from answering the phone at three thirty-three in the morning?"

It's a rhetorical question, a dumb one at that, but I'm allowed at least one per day. And as I shaved, my mind is taken back.

The smell of purple filled the foggy air. My Pendleton shirt was already moist by the time I reached the foothills. My trusty sidekick Trip-a-long couldn't have cared less about the weather. She knew that we'd soon be on the mountain and she'd get to chase rabbits. Her tri-colored fur glistened as I reached down to give her head a scratch. "Go get em, Trip." With that, she tore off, kicking up dirt. I watched as she ran full-throttled with her nose no less than an inch off the ground and her white-tipped tail straight in the air. I had only taken about four steps when I heard her bellow out in hound dog bliss. Little Trip had found herself some rabbits.

Then the memory fades.

Once at work, Bob fills me in. It's worse than I had imagined. Not only are the dealers' communication not getting processed, but the comm queues on the mainframe are also filling up. This event could bring the entire mainframe to its knees.

I get a roll call of what is happening. Around midnight, the communication buffers started backing up. None of the dealers' parts orders can be processed. There are entire, regional, part fulfillment warehouses whose crews are just standing around because the dealer orders haven't come through. No trucks can be loaded, no commerce, people just standing around. Now we are talking about serious money.

Then I get the call. The boss is calling me because everyone is yelling at him. On some cosmic level, I believe this to be a manifestation of corporate gravity. I was at the bottom of that hill. After he has transferred all his shit and just a wee bit more to me, he winds up his rant with, "What's wrong, what are we doing about, and how long will it be before it is fixed?"

There is that awkward silence between us. Then I tell the boss what he wants to hear, "I have everyone working on it. If you get any more calls, to have them call me for status updates."

Translation: I got nothing, and I'll take the flak.

I reach across my desk, grab the stress ball, squeeze it, and drift off again:

On these chilly, misty mornings, we had Cowles Mountain all to ourselves. For miles and miles, it would only be Trip and me. Having played on this hill for years, I knew the shortest way to the top. I start the arduous trek to the peak. I increase my pace, hoping to catch the rising sun.

I knew this mountain. Past explorations had taught me which ravines were passible and which ones ended in unscalable cliffs. Each footfall left an impression on the shallow loam. Each breath tasted of the faint perfume from the purple sagebrush and the damp grasses. This mountain is a land of the hardy chaparral and manzanitas whose branches tore at my flannel shirt as I journeyed up the narrow trails.

Bob's face broke the moment.

"Cary, look at this."

I followed Bob to a terminal hooked up to the satellite system. The screen showed the timeline and the increasing payloads. Seeing this enabled me to put all the pieces into place. I delved deeper into the data, and with a couple of quick calculations, my assumption held. The dealerships had started transmitting on their staggered schedules, yet they never stopped transmitting. As more dealerships across the country came on-line, the problem was going to get worse. I leaned back in my chair to clear my mind for a possible solution.

Again, I heard Trip bellow; only this time, she was much farther off. Rabbits were her life, a time to chase, and howl. Wet mornings like these, Trip would find the rabbits nesting together under the canopy of the sage and chaparral, waiting wide-eyed for the sun to come up. Although hidden from view, the rabbits were beacons for Trip's intrepid nose. Her howl punctuated each discovery and was followed by the chase. Her stout beagle body was perfectly suited to hunting on these trails. Her compact stature allowed her to run thought the sagebrush tunnels that the rabbits had bored like a maze through the underbrush. And her howls trailed off as she ran further and further away.

My boots dug into the steep sides of the ravines. The sandstone ground resisted all attempts of water to penetrate it. My shoes would often slip as I planted my next step. The composition of these steep valleys was little more than decomposing granite and sandstone the consistency of ball bearings on concrete. With two steps forward and one sliding back, I made gradual progress until I finally reached the height of the low hanging fog.

Amongst these clouds, I could barely see. The dew drops settled on my eyelashes in perfect jeweled droplets. It clung to everything, my clothes, face, and hands. I stopped. Dew started falling down my face like saltless tears. I stood so long that the fog began to permeate all my clothing. Eventually motivated by a chill that ran through my body, I continued.

I had the answer. One or more of the dealers' transmissions were looping, stuck in an endless cycle of transmitting, and then re-transmitting ad infinitum. I let Bob know, and we got to work calculating what dealership(s) might be the culprit(s). After we came up with a few possibilities, we remotely signed on to those servers. With most of the satellite's bandwidth consumed, it took forever to get through. We stared at those green screens and waited, hoping we had guessed correctly.

I clambered over a rock outcropping and noticed that the ground rose less gradually. My gait became longer. I knew that I was approaching the top of that ravine. I reached the esplanade. The land became almost level, but the fog obscured my view of the final goal, the rocky pinnacle. Trusting my internal compass, I soldiered upward.

Out of the fog trotted Trip. Her nose would always find me. Her tongue was swinging from side to side. With a slobbering smile, she looked up. I bent down and grabbed my canteen. Into my cupped hand, I poured some water which Trip greedily lapped up. As she drank, I visually checked her over. She smelt like a bundle of burnt sage. Tiny sagebrush leaves covered her coat, and her white legs were now a mixture of reddish dust and dew. After she drank, I scratched her under her chin and stared into her face. She was not done. Nor was I.

"Go git'em" was all that was required to release her back to the wilds. "Go git'em" was what echoed in my mind as I headed toward my goal.

93

Fog muted the colors of the scrubs and brush. It softened their edges. The steeper the hill, the more erosion made it impassable. I took a deep breath and began to hop over the ruts and toward the peak.

Finally, the computer connected to the dealership server. Bob and I let out a muffled yeah. We signed on and brought up the communication subsystems. It felt like an eternity, but when the screen displayed the information, we saw the culprit. A portion of the nightly transmission was repeating. We looked at the job queues, and sure enough, it had spawned hundreds of jobs. The dealer's server was cannibalizing itself to send these transmissions. We shut down those jobs and disabled the processes. Now that we had found the problem, we started to document the interim steps need to get things back into place. Bob passed that information on to our crew. I leaned back in my chair and, for the first time, felt that we had a chance to fix this before it all came crashing down.

Just before reaching the peak, I noticed that I had hiked above the fog.

The vista stretched to the distant ocean. It was a continuous layer of undulating gray-white carpet that blotted out the land and left only fog and bright blue sky. After a few minutes in the sunshine, I took off my Pendleton. With newfound clarity, I saw the peak. In no time, I had clambered up its stony sides and sat down.

As I drank from my canteen, I stood up so that I could take in the entire 360 degree vista. Although the sun had already risen, the trip was well worth the effort. I savored this rare delicacy of a world above the clouds. After a while, my hair was starting to dry under the sun.

I don't know how long I lingered, heck I might still be there today if Trip hadn't found me. She began to bark because she couldn't find her way up the house-size boulders I stood on.

I climbed down a bit, then slid down a bit and ultimately jumped off my perch. Once down, I offered Trip some more water. I took a few more mental snapshots of this alternate world then, with a deep breath, we started back down the mountain.

With everyone's help, we were able to get the dealerships to stop transmitting. The workload on the satellite slowly decreased, and the mainframe was able to catch up. Our triage was successful. We now had the luxury of time to discover the root cause of this fiasco. And for the first time that day, I allowed myself to smile.

As I started walking back down, Trip took the lead. Her little legs trotted in a zigzag pattern about ten yards in front of me. Her nose never more than an inch off the ground and her tail straight in the air. We walked together down into the rolling sea of fog, letting it slowly consume us and consume the sun.

Trip led the way back.

She took the long way home, and that was perfectly fine by me.

Creativity

The world never changes until it is touched

Creativity. What do you think? Some of us have it, and some of us don't. Balderdash! Creativity is a river that runs through each one of us. This river of creativity is merely a reverberation of that single most creative act, the event of creation itself. (Cue the rumbling thunder!)

And although I was not there, I have been told:

From the numb nothingness that never was sprung forth light and life, and all that is was begat from the numb nothingness that never was.

And like creation itself, each of us is born a tabula rasa, a clean slate, an empty page. We are born ready to be filled like an empty garage.

Imagine a blank piece of paper.

Cradling this blank paper like you would a newborn child, look down and say, "Ah, what a beautiful child, he has his father's eyes and his mother's nose. Cute as a button, don't you know!"

But no time to waste, he's off to school.

Our empty page child is off and running. At school, the teacher will place a blank sheet of paper before this child and coax him to write, to draw, to create.

Do you remember how it felt looking down at that blank sheet of paper and feeling dread or even despair? What to draw? What to write? For many of us, this daunting task quickly morphed into I cannot draw, I cannot write.

For the brave among us, we transformed that blank sheet of paper into a doorway, a portal. Once we saw the paper transform, all that remained was for us to follow Alice down that rabbit hole.

Like my pappy said, "Son, this requires less looking and more leapin'."

You dive in.

Once inside this paper-white world, you look around. You swim in a sea of monochromatic redundancy, and white is not even your favorite color. After a few moments, you begin to discern distant snowcapped peaks; you feel the snow's cold, wet kiss. You hear the frictional hiss of the snow blowing over the icy expanse.

Then you meet your first snowbound inhabitant, Shorty. He's a mountain man who offers you shelter from the cold. Through a snowbound door, you follow him into his single room, subterranean domicile. Against the walls, he has stacked boxes and boxes of provisions. On the far wall is a single twin bed. On the opposite wall is a table with three chairs. Shorty offers you a seat and a hot cup of coffee. The aroma of the coffee mingles with the musk of the small room. As you sit and sip, you notice the narrow, slit windows that mark ground level. Snow impacts these windows.

You break the silence by asking your host, "Shorty, what brought you here?"

He pauses and then, with a puzzled look, replies with a laugh, "Why you did!"

Shorty's laughter grows louder and louder until it shatters the narrow windows. Torrents of snow rush in and rapidly fill up the tiny cabin. You watch as the snow engulfs the now white-bearded Shorty until his laughter stops.

You look around, and again everything is white with only your memory colored by the journey. From the numb nothingness of an empty page springs forth light and life.

You can't turn creativity on or turn it off, but a brave soul and stout heart can nurture it. Through each of us runs a river of creativity. We are all anglers on that river's bank, and our catches are always colorful if not always relevant to our immediate needs.

Because each time we cast into that river, we never strike the same place twice. That river is continuously moving, infinitely changing.

But there are forces pitted against you, for instance, that memory of one high school writing assignment that still haunts you.

You poured out your thoughts on that white parchment — feelings rooted in the fertile grounds of your angst. You hand the assignment in to your teacher. She returns the document to you with a poisoned salutation, "Well, it's a fascinating story, but it's a bit too dark. The best I can give you is C."

You take the story back. To you, it was a catharsis; it was a step toward corralling your inner demons. But to someone else, it was only a C paper.

Just remember that everything you create takes you one step closer to the highest you. Each venture with the pen or the brush changes you, changes your trajectory, and improves your destiny. Creativity is that river that runs through you, and from this river comes your nourishment.

Now the next time you investigate that blank piece of paper, pause and see how the limitlessness of the numb nothingness that never was has brought forth light and life.

And when you decide to leap, I will see you all on the other side of the empty page.

Chapter 8:

PERSONAL GROWTH

Our persona is not some static portrait like that of Dorian Gray. Nope, we are constantly changing, constantly buffeted by internal and external forces, from the loss of loved ones to those occasional bloody noses that reorient us. Change is a teacher in many guises. We cannot stop change, I know because I've tried, but we can sure learn from it.

Canvas

Tears teach us what needs to be released

On a visit to the Norton Simon Museum, I chanced by Van Gogh, The Mulberry Tree. Before this eternal masterpiece, I sat and let the full effect of its three-dimensional visuals permeate my entire being. After a while, I saw, then, felt the master's work come into me as a sensation that has persisted the relentless destruction of time. It was just me and the distillation of truth and beauty that hangs before me.

Absorbed at that moment, I remembered that through x-ray technology, modern curators have discovered that some of the masters re-used their canvases. That made me wonder, what is buried beneath the masterpiece that we now see? For although we are awed by the master's work, we are ignorant of what came before, what lies beneath.

That knowledge exploded an epiphany that caused the blood to rush from my face.

You see, I was an angry child who grew into a furious young man. My father's legacy was that men never cried. Men faced their foes. Instead of tears, I learned to use my fists. I would fight rather than back down or cry. I preferred to knock heads than run away. I would fight until I either left boasting or bloodied.

And I would not cry. No, never cry. Never back down.

Was it my tolerance for pain or my stubborn defiance never to be a victim? Eventually, my foolish fearlessness never to back down morphed into my unflinching ability to look long and hard at what others would avoid.

Decent society would turn their heads when the drug-addled homeless would walk by, but for me, it was a sign of cowardice to look away. I would study their weather-worn visages, their grime encrusted fingers, their unsteady staggers, and their peculiar aroma. I never would look away from these societal roadkills. And I never looked away from my own bloodied face.

Never looking away and never backing down from the decay and the dirt of society, I grew hard, and I grew alone. I kept my emotional distance until the simplest of things whacked my fragile world off its unreachable shelf.

I was running a 10k down in Chula Vista. I was on pace for a personal best. I rounded the corner and came stride for stride with a wheelchair participant. His arms expanded and contracted like the breathing bag they attempted to resuscitate my grandfather with just before he died. His gloves showed the absorption from his bloody, blistered hands, but his face showed pride, not pain.

My feeble, "All right man," as I passed him, was returned with a smile and a nod of appreciation.

Thank god the sweat would hide my tears. Tears that no blow to my body had ever elicited. Tears for the power of that man's human spirit. The spirit to knock down the gates of hell, the courage to rattle the gates of heaven. A man who repainted his life after the loss of his legs. A man shining with the spirit and truth of a new masterpiece. A masterpiece on wheels for all of us to see. A snapshot of what we can accomplish, what we can overcome.

I began to repaint my world. I began to observe my anger with the same unflinching vision that I had cast outward. I now looked deep within and discovered the societal roadkill that lurked inside me. I could now begin to heal my scars with this newfound courage of introspection. This courage allowed me to improve and learn to connect emotionally.

I am just a work in progress. We are all just unfinished masterpieces. With each stroke of the brush, we create anew and forever alter the canvas of our lives. We paint with a palette of pleasure and pain. Our life is a single canvas that contains layers upon buried layers of past works. All incarnations include flaws. All of our masterpieces encapsulate the weight of our darkness and the lightness of our spirit. As our masterworks hang before us, we must try hard not to look away. Our flaws contain a unique power. Once observed, they empower us to pick up the brush again and toil to repaint a new masterpiece.

Sitting in the museum, with past master's work before me, I realized that everyone I meet is a work in progress who is painted again and again on their own solitary canvas.

Three Doors

Come on down!

Would you like to have what is behind: door number one, door number two, or door number three?

Yes, some of us may recall the old Monty Hall's, Let's Make a Deal.

Ponder for a moment all the thresholds you have crossed. Each has a door, usually a closed door, and a question. Should you open that door, or should you turn and walk away.

Every life has thousands of doors. Here are three doors that have helped define me:

I remember the first one just like it was just yesterday.

I am the child of a navy man, which meant that we moved every two to three years, from the west coast to the east coast. Our family repeated this peripatetic cycle again and again.

As a child in the second grade, I can remember being the new kid in a new town walking into a new school. Walking up to that door and wondering what is behind it. What am I going to see? Are they going to like me? Are they going to make fun of me? Or will it be a place of excitement, a place where I can make new friends? As I grasp the doorknob, fear, and anxiety fill my tiny body. But I walk through that gateway because I gotta find out.

The second door was more massive yet. At the end of a long hospital corridor, my wife and I stood for a moment. We looked at each other and steeled our demeanor as I grasped the handle.

A phone call from my sister had brought us before that steel door. My two-year-old niece had to have emergency head surgery. It was late when my wife and I arrived.

Standing before her hospital door, we imaged the worst. I grasped that door handle, and I forced myself to hope for the best. I then turned the handle, and we walked in.

In that dimly lit room, we found little Cassie standing, clutching the side of her crib. And from across the darkened room, all we saw was her smile beaming out. A bright and innocent smile that contrasted with the dark cross stitching that ran from ear to ear across the top of her swollen and shaved head.

We brought her a stuffed animal that we hoped would ease her distress. Before she received our token, she bestowed upon us a smile, a smile of recognition, a smile of resilience. We talked to her, telling her how happy we were to see her. We told her what a strong girl she was. Her smile uplifted our voices and gave us strength.

After a while, my sister and brother-in-law returned, and we left Cassie to her parents. As the door shut behind us, we cried, touched by her smile and bounce in such circumstances. Cassie had taught us a valuable lesson. She taught us that it does not matter what you go through; it matters what you make of it.

The last door did not appear for many years. Surrounded by beautiful paintings and sculptures, we walked down the long halls of the hospice center. Behind this door was only the preamble of death. Together Marge and I opened it and discovered something nobler than death. We found my father-in-law, who held his wife's hand while he stroked and comforted her with gentle words and a feather touch. He murmured to Phyllis. In the effort to be strong, my wife fought back the tears as she hugged her dad.

No other words were necessary, just waiting. Marge's dad taught us that there is something higher than death. We found it behind that door. Behind death's door, we found love and life.

Three doors, just three out of thousands of doors. What could walking through a door mean? It could mean nothing, or it could mean everything.

It is what you feel and what you learn by boldly going, regardless of your doubt and anxiety. Open a door and experience the universe beyond.

Door number one, door number two, or door number three, it's your life, and you get to choose.

Step on through to the other side.

Just One More

All I can do is one, and that is all it takes to move mountains

At four-forty each workday morning, my watch alarm goes off. In under a nanosecond, my wife mumbles, "Turn it off and get your ass out of bed."

Her encouraging words start me staggering towards the bathroom. With one eye open, I shave. By the time I get the other eye open, I've finished dressing in my gym clothes. Picking up my racquetball bag, I am out the door and off to the gym.

It's always dark when I get to the West End gym, yet the parking lot is surprisingly full. I check-in at the front desk and walk back to the racquetball courts. Once inside, I turn the morning news on and start stretching. Ever since I was a wrestler in high school, when my coach would always scream, "You gotta stretch before you sweat," I stretch as much to loosen up as I do to take inventory of what part of my body is working on that day.

I stretch my back. Check, it's working. Stretch my legs. Check, they are working. Stretch my shoulders. Check, they are working. And on down the line.

Now between each stretch, I find myself in a prone position on the floor. About a year ago, while down on the carpet, I decided to add a single push-up to my stretching routine. Stretch one leg, then do one push-up, stretch my other leg, one push-up, stretch my back, then one push-up until I had fully stretched and completed eight single push-ups. By the eighth push-up, my arms were shaking.

I kept doing that one push-up, and after a month, I noticed that my last push-up had become as easy as my first. That got me thinking. I decided that I'd do just one more.

Now the routine was stretch, two push-ups, stretch, two push-ups, stretch, two push-ups until I had completed stretching. By then end of that routine, I could not even finish my last two push-ups. The game was now afoot.

A couple of months later, I again discovered that my last two push-ups were as easy as my first two, so I added just one more.

Throughout that year, as my body adapted to the increasing resistance, I kept increasing my pushups by just one more. And as if by magic, I now do ten push-ups throughout my stretching routine for a total of eighty push-ups each morning before I play racquetball.

Eighty push-ups were never my goal. If I had even considered such a feat, I would have never begun. For me, eighty push-ups would be akin to standing face to face with an African elephant, a fork in one hand and a knife in the other and saying to the elephant, "You are what's for dinner."

There is not a less daunting number than one. Everyone can do just one of something. You can do one, and he can do one, and she can do one. Everyone can do one something each day. And over time, a one percent improvement each day can lead you to a three hundred and sixty percent improvement over the year. That equates to a thirty-six times better you.

Now the science/magic of just one more applies to just about everything that you currently find outside of your grasp — learning a new hobby, writing your family stories down, learning a new career. Just one each day is the simple yet radical way to change the arc of your life.

Then just one more.

Weightless

It's not what humanity can do; it is what humanity can become

In the late 1920s, the boyhood version of my ninety-four-year-old dad was awestruck by a vision in the verdant valley below. Three locomotives pulled a veritable country mile of goods before him. The black smoke, its piercing whistle, and the thundering rumble of the ground beneath his feet spoke to him of a power beyond his backwoods imagination. In the 1920s, these trains were the standard of power and might.

In the late 1960's you would have found me in my pajamas sitting way too close to our black and white television. There I marveled as the Saturn 5 launched from Cape Canaveral, hypnotized as this skyscraper rocket tore the surly bonds of earth and rent the sky asunder.

The power of man's mechanical ability increases exponentially every generation. Yet quite by accident, I discovered the most powerful thing man has ever created. It has no moving parts, requires no factory for production, and is invisible. Although weightless, it has the power to move the world.

It was a Sunday, and my wife and I had just completed work on our rental property when we decided to have something to eat. Over in Gardena, there is this little place called The Pan. It is an old nineteen-fifties soda joint that has been hipsterized.

At The Pan, there are some inside tables, there are some outside tables, and there are some in-and-outside tables. Nonetheless, on Sunday,

108

there are never enough tables. We gave our name to the hostess and discovered that the wait would be about thirty minutes. We grabbed the last seats in the shade and waited for our turn.

As we talked, we both noticed a young couple standing out in the parking lot. They looked to be in their late twenties or early thirties. The young man stood very close to his spouse, who was very, very pregnant. Standing on the scorching asphalt is no place for a very, very pregnant woman to be. I nodded to Marge, who nodded back in agreement. I then got up and approached the couple.

I said hello and offered them our seats in the shade because the asphalt is way too hot. He said, "Nah, Nah," yet with a bit more insistence, they complied. We introduced ourselves as Cary and Marge; they were Tom and Sue.

We congratulated them on their upcoming birth and learned that Sue was literally, I mean minute-to-minute, ready to deliver.

"Today could be the day," Tom said.

As his wife carefully sat down, holding her belly, Marge got up to let the Tom sit next to her. The young gentleman thanked her but would not take Marge's seat in the shade. So, my wife sat down next to Sue, and they immediately bonded.

As Tom and I stood in the parking lot, I asked Tom, "How are you holding up?"

"Good, good; I've got the baby's room ready…we're having a girl. We finished all our classes, and I've got her mother on speed dial".

As he talked, it brought me way back to when we had our first child. Now when I say we, I mean my wife, because I had only an ancillary part in the process. Talking with Tom brought back my fears of being a good dad, and the anxiety of planning a secure future, and just being a whole lot more, dare I say it, responsible. My mind flashed back to all those good times, those hard questions, and crucial conversations. Of having to walk the tightrope roles of friend, mentor, and parental unit. I told Tom that he'd be a great dad.

And then I leaned into him and whispered, "Being a dad is the absolute hardest job you'll ever love."

Tom thought for a moment and then smiled.

We talked a bit more when I heard the hostess call "Kellems, party of two."

Marge stood up, we congratulated them on their new life and walked into the restaurant.
We talked as we enjoyed The Pan's unique twist on breakfast. Before we knew it, Marge got a box to go, and I asked for the bill. That's when the server said, "Already paid for."

Momentarily unable to process what she said, I asked, "What?"

The server smiled and said that a young couple had paid for our bill when they left—paid in full!

That's when it struck me. Time just stopped. Their act of kindness and generosity was weightless. Kindness and generosity are like air, but the power behind them is mightier than a train traveling across the plains or a rocket blasting into space.

This act took us to this moment to process and brought us closer together. It wasn't the money at all, it was the fact that someone took the time to thank us, never needing thanks in return.

And for us, those are the most potent things that humankind has created: kindness and generosity. They are weightless yet powerful, all at once.

Lessons from a Bloody Nose

Irish blood is as intoxicating as a robust single malt

I became a high school wrestler because the football coach didn't want to be responsible for telling my mother that a baby Samoan linebacker nicknamed "Tonage" had interred my ninety-five-pound body a foot beneath the forty-yard line. "Tonage" was twice my weight and half-again my height and would grow up to fill an eight-foot doorway.

Utilizing the same audacity that allowed a ninety-five-pound kid to believe he could be a football player, I started wrestling at the age of thirteen. I was lucky enough to get on a team that was in desperate need of a body to fill the under one-hundred-pound weight class. I was the right kid in the right place. I went to practice each day and worked through the grueling workouts. With all the intensity of a caged animal, I went at whoever the coach sent my way.

But even in wrestling, ambition and strength will only get you so far. To some of my fellow wrestlers, I was like a hungry weasel chewing on the leg of a T-Rex. Not a real threat, just a slight annoyance.

After a week of practice, I had plenty of bruises and mat burns, but no form. The coach said I needed a wrestling buddy, someone who would show me the ropes. After that Friday's practice, he hooked me up with Ernie. To my good fortune, Ernie was just about my size. (Coach called us squatty bodies because we were in the lowest weight classes.) Ernie gave me a critical eye, extended his hand in what seemed like a gentlemanly gesture. I took his hand, and he immediately pulled my arm across his body so that he could take me down from behind. After I was on the mat, he looked down at me and said, "Lesson one."

Ernie was a tough kid from the rough streets of Logan Heights. For the next couple of weeks, he did his best to beat me down. Let me rephrase that, Ernie beat the living daylights out of me. In the process, he showed me every trick that he had learned. Even the dirty ones that ruptured my nose into a bloody mess.

But Ernie did not know I had a secret weapon; I was an angry and very stubborn kid.

Just ask my mom or my older sisters who would say, "Oh, he's a good boy, but he can be stubborn."

Translation: I was stubborn. Irish stubborn. Once I got something in my head, stand back or get knocked down.

As the season progressed, I got better. Because of Ernie's merciless tutelage, I got better fast. My technique improved. Hell, it had to improve to prevent further beatings. And by the end of the season, I could hold my own against Ernie. Which, by the way, just pissed him off. His merciless mentorship had the unintended consequence of also forcing him to get better.

By the end of that first season, I was winning most of my league matches. Our lower weight classes became formidable. I wrestled at ninety-five pounds, Ernie at 105 and Joe at 115. We dominated our league, and we were only freshmen.

Although we were from different parts of town, we became fast friends. During the offseason, we started to do things together. Ernie invited us to his sister's quinceañera. Joe invited us over to help him rebuild the carburetor in an old Ford that would become his first car. And I convinced them to go for a hike, a merciless hike of subtle revenge.

On the mat, we fought each other. We pushed each other in our workouts. We even started going to the local community college to practice with their team. By our junior year, we were some of the best in our city. All because we held each other to a standard.

I pushed us to a standard of strength.

Joe pushed us to a standard of finesse.

And Ernie pushed us to a standard of cocky quickness.

Who holds you to a standard? Who pushes you to be better?

Who?

Long Bar

Mr. Pavlov was right, yet it was the dogs
who learned the lesson best

I don't care how bad you are feeling, if you look down an see a furry bundle of bouncing excitement replete with a wet nose, bright eyes, and a tail-wagging to the beat of a heavy metal tempo, you are just going to feel better because it's all about puppy love.

Mr. Pavlov's research in the field of classical conditioning taught us the power of external stimuli via a dinner bell and a meal.

I am here to tell you that it's the dogs who have put Mr. Pavlov's research to best use. When you see that bounding bundle of a puppy, you can't resist. You must hug, hold, and love them. And for those of us lucky enough to have lived with a dog, puppy love never dies.

Knowing the awesome power that a puppy exudes, it is almost understandable why a group of slightly inebriated college guys would turn to the dark world of international puppy smuggling. We would have done almost anything to get our cute contraband across the Mexican border that night.

Crammed amongst us four guys in 1972, VW Bug was that contraband puppy. As our car chugged towards the San Ysidro checkpoint, our laughter about our predicament turned to sweat. In a time when carrying drugs across the Mexican border would get you a forty-year stint in the big house, we were sure that smuggling a puppy could end our sorry butts inside a Mexican jail surrounded by the ominous laughter of our guards.

The closer we got, the sharper our peril came into focus. In front of us, we could see the border agents wave each vehicle up. Then he would bend down and stick his head into the cars looking for contraband. Moments later, the agent would either motion the driver on through to San Diego or send him to be scrutinized closer than a bikini-clad babe during Naval Fleet week.

We knew it. We were going to spend the rest of our lives in a foreign jail.

That's when the puppy began to welp for attention. Sweat began to roll down our faces like the condensation on a glass of cold beer on a hot day.

Car by car, we inched closer and closer to the burly border officer until our court date with destiny arrived. At practically the same instant that the checkpoint officer stuck his head into our vehicle, Mike shoved the puppy under his hoodie.

The officer smiled a devious smile and said, "How's it going, guys? Got anything to declare?"

In a moment of silence that felt like it surpassed two eternities, I choked out a feeble, "Nothing but a great time, officer."

With that frail quip, the guys erupted into nervous laughter. Laughter loud enough to mask the puppy's pleas.

A far-off twinkle in his eye, the officer, waves us on toward San Diego with a warning to be safe.

Mere seconds beyond the border agent's earshot, Mike let the puppy out from under his hoodie, and he pranced about the backseat yelping with glee and licking our noses. We all yelled in relief.

That's when Mike shouted, "Hey, what is his name gonna be?"

The silence of drunken thought ensued until John broke out, "Long Bar. His name will be Long Bar."

The name stuck. It was entirely appropriate because that was the name of the Tijuana dive bar where he found us that night.

Within the hour, we were home. We opened the door, and Long Bar just made himself at home. Before crashing into bed, we put some leftovers on the floor for our new addition to eat, and we passed out on our respective beds.

In the harsh light of the morning after, we rose to the prancing, dancing of our cute little puppy. As I looked down through morning eyes, I was shocked to discover that our sweet little puppy was just an old dog. Long Bar's smile betrayed missing teeth; his snout was graying and missing a whisker or two. His energetic demeanor had not waned. He ran in and out between my legs showing the excitement that only a puppy could produce.

Not that it would have taken the wiles of a Mata Hari to deceive a bunch of inebriated college students, but we had risked time in a Tijuana jail for an old dog.

Long Bar spent many years with us in that Santee frat house. All our girlfriends loved him. Heck, they loved him all the more after hearing the story of his abduction and our stupidity. Long Bar grew fat, living off the scraps of my classmates and friends. He mingled during the keg parties. With a dance and a wiggle, he'd cast a spell on each party goer.

In the physical sense, Long Bar is long gone, having lived a comfortable life amongst the rotating college crowd. Yet within me, Long Bar will never die. I see him every morning in my graying muzzle. He is there to reminds me to take on the day with all the enthusiasm that this old dog can muster.

EPILOGUE

THIS BAR

*If you look around the poker table and you can't find the sucker,
find another table*

God walks into this bar. And let me tell you, she is drop-dead gorgeous.

I mean, every eye in the place is on her as she floats through the bar like a dandelion seed on a gentle breeze.

And she is feeling pretty good about herself. And why not? From the numb nothingness that never was, she created all this and more — brains and beauty, whoa, it's no wonder why St. Peter and St. Paul are staring at her.

St. Peter turns to St. Paul and says, "Hey, Paulie is youss thinkin', what I'm thinkin'?"

St. Paul gulps down his drink and says,

"Well, then Peter me lad, we are both going to Hell in a handbasket!"

When she gets to the bar, she sits down. After a moment, she starts to strum her fingers and then finally says,

"Jesus Christ...what does it take for God to get a drink in this place?"

Right then and there, the bartender turns around. It's none other than Jesus "Water into Wine" Christ himself. He smiles and pours her a double.

She takes it and drinks it on down. A faint smile crosses her face. But it doesn't last long.

Lucifer walks into this very same bar. And he looks like he just walked off the cover of GQ. He looks like a young George Clooney. Heck, it is George Clooney. Yep, Mr. Clooney is the devil himself. And he is feeling pretty good too. And why not, the devil started as a lowly fruit peddler in the garden of Eden, and now he's CEO of a massive empire with minions throughout eternity.

As the Dark Angel, he is sporting a fat cigar. He offers you an irresistible deal because he knows that you are damned if you do and damned if you don't. Then he leans back, smiles, and wonders how he got such a fantastic job.

About that time, he notices the beauty sitting at the bar. And he knows, he just knows that she's going to be going home with him tonight. He walks on up and whispers over her shoulder, "Hey baby, did you hurt yourself when you fell from heaven?"

God turns around and says, "Lucifer, I'd tell you to go to Hell, but you are already there. So shut up, sit down, and have a drink."

A bit crestfallen, Lucifer pulls up the barstool next to her and sits down. Jesus brings him his regular.

You walk into this very same bar and heck everyone knows your name and everything is so familiar, and why not, this bar is you. It is the watering hole of those competing forces that exists within every one of us. It is where the God within you can sit down and shares a drink and some conversation with your darker side.

Every one of you is a unique cocktail composed of creativity and logic, some love and a little hate, some fire, and ice. So, come right up and order yourself a drink and share some conversation.

Whatever you order, take a moment and savor the duality of the cocktail that is uniquely you.

And for Christ's sake, don't forget to tip the bartender.

ABOUT THE AUTHOR

Cary T. Kellems is a husband, father, retired IBM IT Architect, and reluctant cat-lover. A Distinguished Toastmaster and prolific public speaker known for his energetic storytelling style; he has given over 100 presentations to various groups.

As both a speaker and a writer, Cary draws on his experiences growing up in an military family, coming of age as a young man living in Southern California, and working as a technology professional to weave captivating stories that illuminate the human condition.

He is one of the co-authors in *Rough Writers 2019 Anthology, Moments in Space & Time* Within each of Cary's stories is a seed of self-awareness. Please read his work as encouragement for you to take up your pen and slay your own inner obstacles.

Intrigued? For more stories or information, please visit Cary's website at www.murphyslawtoenlightenment.com.

www.ingramcontent.com/pod-product-compliance
Lightning Source LLC
Chambersburg PA
CBHW060018050426
42448CB00012B/2804